IPv6: The New Internet Protocol

Christian Huitema

For book and bookstore information

http://www.prenhall.com

Prentice Hall PTR
Upper Saddle River, New Jersey 07458

Library of Congress Cataloging-in-Publication Data
Huitema, Christian.
    IPv6--The New Internet Protocol / Christian Huitema
        p. cm.
    Includes index.
    ISBN 0-13-241936-X
    1. Internet (Computer network) 2. Computer network protocols. I. Title.
TK5105.875.I57H78   1996
004.6'2--dc20   95-43479
                                                 CIP

Editorial/production supervision: *Joanne Anzalone*
Manufacturing manager: *Alexis Heydt*
Acquisitions editor: *Mary Franz*
Editorial assistant: *Noreen Regina*
Cover design: *Design Source*
Cover Design Direction: *Jerry Votta*
Art Director: *Gail Cocker-Bogusz*
Cover Art: "Image of A Sunrise:" *Carr Clifton*

© 1996 by Prentice Hall PTR
Prentice-Hall, Inc.
A Simon & Schuster Company
Upper Saddle River, New Jersey 07458

The publisher offers discounts on this book when ordered in bulk quantities.
For more information, contact:

> Corporate Sales Department
> PTR Prentice Hall
> 1 Lake Street
> Upper Saddle River, NJ 07458
>
> Phone: 800-382-3419, Fax: 201-592-2249
> E-mail: dan_rush@prenhall.com

Printed in the United States of America
10 9 8 7 6 5 4 3 2 1

ISBN **0-13-241936-X**

Prentice-Hall International (UK) Limited, *London*
Prentice-Hall of Australia Pty. Limited, *Sydney*
Prentice-Hall Canada Inc., *Toronto*
Prentice-Hall Hispanoamericana, S.A., *Mexico*
Prentice-Hall of India Private Limited, *New Delhi*
Prentice-Hall of Japan, Inc., *Tokyo*
Simon & Schuster Asia Pte. Ltd., *Singapore*
Editora Prentice-Hall do Brasil, Ltda., *Rio de Janeiro*

Contents

Introduction

On a Saturday in June 1992, I took a plane at Osaka airport. I was leaving Kobe, where I had taken part in the first congress of the Internet Society. The Internet Activities Board (IAB) met in parallel with that congress. Shortly after the plane took off, I opened my portable computer and started to write the draft of the recommendation that we just had adopted. The choice of 32-bit addresses may have been a good decision in 1978, but the address size was proving too short. The Internet was in great danger of running out of network numbers, the routing tables were getting too large, there was even a risk of running out of addresses altogether. We had to work out a solution, we needed a new version of the Internet protocol, and we needed it quite urgently. During the meeting, we had managed to convince ourselves that this new version could be built out of CLNP, the Connection-Less Network Protocol defined by the ISO as part of the Open System Interconnection architecture. The draft that I was writing was supposed to explain all this: that we wanted to retain the key elements of the Internet Architecture, that we would only use CLNP as a strawman, that we would indeed upgrade it to fit our needs, that we hoped to unite the community behind a single objective, to focus the effort and guarantee the continued growth of the Internet.

1.1 Preparing for a Decision

I wrote the first draft in the plane and posted it to our internal distribution list the next Monday. The IAB discussed it extensively. In less than two weeks, it went through eight successive revisions. We thought that our wording was very careful, and we were prepared to discuss it and try to convince the Internet community. Then, everything accelerated. Some journalists got the news, an announcement was hastily written, and many members of the community felt betrayed. They perceived that we were selling the Internet to the ISO, that headquarters was simply giving the field to an enemy that they had fought for many years and eventually vanquished. The IAB had no right to take such a decision alone. Besides, CLNP was a pale imitation of IP. It had been designed 10 years ago, and the market had failed to pick it up for all those years. Why should we try to resurrect it?

The IAB announcement was followed by a tremendous hubbub in the Internet's electronic lists. The IAB draft was formally withdrawn a few weeks later, during the July 1992 meeting of the Internet Engineering Task Force (IETF). The incident triggered a serious reorganization of the whole IETF decision process, revising the role of managing bodies such as the Internet Engineering Steering Group (IESG) or the Internet Architecture Board, the new appellation of the IAB. The cancellation of the IAB decision also opened a period of competition. Several teams tried to develop their own solutions to the Internet's crisis and proposed their own version of the new Internet Protocol. The IESG organized these groups in a specific area, managed by two co-directors, Scott Bradner and Alison Mankin. In addition to the competing design groups, the area included specific working groups trying to produce an explicit requirement document or to assess the risk by getting a better understanding of the Internet's growth. A directorate was named. Its members were various experts from different sectors of the Internet community, including large users as well as vendors and scientists. The directorate would serve as a jury for the evaluation of the different proposals.

The most visible part of the decision process was an estimation of the future size of the Internet. That effort started in fact in 1991, at the initiative of the IAB. We all agreed, as a basic hypothesis, that the Internet should connect all the computers in the world. There are about 200 million of them today, but the number is growing rapidly. Vast portions of the planet are getting richer and more industrialized. There are reasons to believe that at some point in the near future all Indian schoolboys and all Chinese schoolgirls will use their own laptop computers at school. In fact, when we plan the new Internet, it would be immoral not to do so as if all humans would be eventually connected. According to the population growth estimates available in 1992, it would mean about 10 billion people by the year 2020. But, then, each human is very likely to be served by more than one computer. We already find computers in cars, and we will find them in domestic equipment such as refrigerators or washing machines. All these computers could be connected to the Internet. A computer in your car could send messages to the service station, warning that the brakes should be repaired. Your pacemaker could send an alarm message to your cardiologist when some bizarre spikes are noticed. We could even find microscopic computers in every light bulb so that we could switch off the light by sending a message over the Internet. A figure of a hundred computers per human is not entirely unrealistic, leading to a thousand billion computers in the Internet in 2020. But some have observed that such a target was a bit narrow, that we wanted safety margins. Eventually, the official objectives for IPng were set to 1 quadrillion computers (10 to the power 15) connected through 1 trillion networks (10 to the power 12).

A precise survey of the Internet growth quickly taught us that there was no real risk of running out of addresses in the next few years, even if 32-bit addresses only allow us to number 4 billion computers. We get estimates of the number of allocated addresses every month. If we plot them on a log scale and try to prolongate the curve, we see that it crosses the theoretical maximum of 4 billion somewhere between 2005 and 2015. This should give us ample time to develop the new protocol that we were at the time calling IPng (Internet Protocol, new generation). But we should take into account the limited efficiency of address allocation procedures. I proposed to estimate this efficiency through the H ratio:

$$H = \frac{\log (\text{number of addresses})}{\text{number of bits}}$$

The H ratio is defined as the division of the base 10 logarithm of the number of addressed points in the network by the size of the address, expressed in bits. If allocation were perfect, 1 bit would number 2 hosts, 10 bits would number 1024 hosts, and so on. The ratio would be equal to the logarithm of 2 in base 10, which is about 0.30103. In practice, the allocation is never perfect. Each layer of hierarchy contributes to some degree to the inefficiency. The logarithmic nature of the ratio tries to capture this multiplicative effect. Practical observation shows that H varies between 0.22 and 0.26 in large networks, reflecting the degree of efficiency that can be achieved in practice, today.

If the H ratio may vary between 0.22 and 0.26, 32-bit addresses can number between 11 and 200 million hosts. We should keep this in mind. The current Internet protocol is adequate for connecting all the computers of the world today, but it will have almost no margin left at that stage. Predicting a date of 2005 or 2015 simply means that we do not expect a rush into the Internet in the next years. We may well be wrong. In fact, I hope that we will be wrong, that there will indeed be a rush to connect to the Internet.

The other lesson that we can draw from the H ratio is that if we want to connect 1 quadrillion computers to the new Internet, addresses should be at least 68 bits wide for a ratio of 0.22 and only 57 bits wide for a ratio of 0.26. We used this figure when making the final selection.

1.2 Two Years of Competition

When the IAB met in Kobe, there were only three candidate proposals for the new IP. The proposal to use CLNP was known as TUBA (TCP and UDP over Bigger Addresses). The main difference between IP and CLNP was CLNP's 20-octet Network Service Access Point addresses (NSAP). This would certainly suffice for numbering 1 trillion networks. The main argument of this proposal was its installed base. CLNP and companion protocols such as IS-IS for routing were already specified and deployed. A side effect was to allow convergency between the OSI and Internet suites. TCP, UDP, and the ISO transport would all run over CLNP; the protocol wars would be over. The main counterarguments are that this deployment is very limited and that CLNP is a very old and inefficient protocol. It is in fact a copy of IP, the result of an early attempt to get IP standardized within the ISO. During this standardization process, many IP features were corrected, or rather changed, in a way that did not please the Internet community. A slower but more robust checksum algorithm was selected. The alignment of protocol fields on a 32-bit word boundary was lost, as well as some of the key services provided by

ICMP. In the end, this proposal failed because its proponents tried to remain rigidly compatible with the original CLNP specification. They did not change CLNP to incorporate any of the recent improvements to IP, such as multicast, mobility, or resource reservation. They did not want to loose the "installed base" argument, even if that base was in fact quite slim.

In June 1992, Robert Ullman's proposal, called IP version 7, was already available. This proposal evolved between 1992 and 1994. The name was changed to TP/IX in 1993. The new name reflected the desire to change the Transport Control Protocol, TCP, at the same time as the Internet Protocol. It included hooks for speeding up the processing of packets, as well as a new routing protocol called RAP. The proposal failed however to gain momentum and remained quite marginal in the IETF. It evolved in 1994 into a new proposal called CATNIP, which attempted to define a common packet format that would be compatible with IP and CLNP, as well as with Novell's IPX. The proposal had some interesting aspects, but the IPng directorate felt that it was not sufficiently complete at the time of the decision, in July 1994.

The third alternative available in June 1992 was called IP in IP. It proposed to run two layers of the Internet protocol, one for a worldwide backbone and another in limited areas. By January 1993, this proposal had evolved into a new proposal called IP Address Encapsulation, IPAE, that was then adopted as the transition strategy for Simple IP or SIP, which Steve Deering had proposed in November 1992. SIP was essentially a proposal to increase the IP address size to 64 bits and to clean up several of the details of IP that appear obsolete. It used encapsulations rather than options and made packet fragmentation optional. SIP immediately gathered the adherence of several vendors and experimenters. In September 1993, it merged with another proposal called Pip. With Pip, Paul Francis proposed a very innovative routing strategy based on lists of routing directives. This allowed a very efficient implementation of policy routing and also eased the implementation of mobility. The result of the merging between SIP and Pip was called Simple IP Plus, SIPP. It tried to retain the coding efficiency of SIP and the routing flexibility of Pip.

The IPng directorate reviewed all these proposals in June 1994 and published its recommendation in July 1994. It suggested using SIPP as the basis for the new IP, but changing some key features of its design. In particular, they were unhappy with the lists of 64-bit addresses used by SIPP. The new IP would have 128-bit addresses. It will be version 6 of the Internet protocol, following version 4 that is currently in use. The number 5 could not be used because it had been allocated to ST, an experimental "stream" protocol designed to carry real-time services in parallel with IP. The new protocol will be called IPv6.

1.3 The New Specifications

It took a year after the July 1994 decision to finalize the specifications of IPv6. The purpose of this book is to present this new Internet Protocol. The book is organized into eight chapters, including this introduction and a provisional conclusion.

We will start in Chapter 2 by presenting the protocol itself, as well as the new version of the Internet Control Message Protocol, and explaining how Steve Deering and the members of the working group exploited the opportunity to design a new protocol. We avoided most of the second design syndrome effect, kept the proliferation of options and niceties to a minimum, and in fact produced a new Internet Protocol that should be simpler to program and more efficient than the previous version. We will then analyze, in Chapter 3, the evolution of addressing and routing, presenting the various address formats, the supports for multicast and provider addressing.

The three following chapters will be devoted to the new capabilities of IPv6: autoconfiguration, security and the support of real-time communication. All these functionalities could only be partially integrated in IPv4. They will be mandatory in all implementations of IPv6. Chapter 7 will describe the deployment strategy, explaining the transition of the Internet from IPv4 to IPv6.

1.4 Points of Controversy

In theory, the adoption of IPv6 was a miracle of consensus building. The debates were fair, and everybody was supposed to smile after the decision. The members of the SIPP working group tried to play by the rule. They held a party shortly after the decision, but there was no mention of a victory. Officially, it was the "we can't call that winning" party.

In fact, the consensus was quite large. Many members of the TUBA working group joined the IPv6 effort and took part in the final discussions of the specifications. Ross Callon, the very person who forged the TUBA acronym, co-chaired the IPv6 working group with

Steve Deering. But a large consensus is not equivalent to unanimity. Many IETF members still believe that their pet ideas have not been taken into account. Many decisions were only adopted after long discussions, and some points are still debated. I have tried to present these at the end of each chapter in a separate section, Points of Controversy.

1.5 Further Reading

Each chapter ends with a list of references for further reading. Many of these references are Request for Comments (RFC). The RFC series is the electronic publication of reference of the IETF. RFCs are freely available from a number of repositories around the Internet. Some of the references have yet to be published. Provisional versions can be found in the Internet Draft repositories of the IETF.

The IETF decision itself is documented in RFC 1719. Scott Bradner and Alison Mankin, the chairs of the IPng area of the IETF, have been careful to also publish most of the discussion papers as RFC. The TUBA proposal is documented in RFC 1347, 1526, and 1561, Pip in RFC 1621 and 1622, TP/IX in RFC 1475, Catnip in RFC 1707, and SIPP in RFC 1710. Contributions to the debate may be found in RFC 1667 to 1683, 1686 to 1688, 1705 and 1715. Scott and Allison recently edited a book, *IPng Internet Protocol Next Generation* published by Addison-Wesley, that provides an easy to read summary of these discussions.

Readers are expected to be familiar with TCP-IP. Many books have been written to present this technology, notably *Internetworking with TCP-IP* by Douglas E. Comer, published by Prentice Hall.

The Design of IPv6

T he new IP is based on a very simple philosophy: the Internet could not have been so successful in the past years if IPv4 had contained any major flaw. IPv4 was a very good design, and IPv6 should indeed keep most of its characteristics. In fact, it could have been sufficient to simply increase the size of addresses and to keep everything else unchanged. However, 10 years of experience brought lessons. IPv6 is built on this additional knowledge. It is not a simple derivative of IPv4, but a definitive improvement.

2.1 The IPv6 Header Format

Any presentation of the new IP has to start with a presentation of the IPv6 header format. Its is composed of a 64-bit header, followed by two 128-bit IPv6 addresses for source and destination, for a total length of 40 bytes.

The initial 64 bits comprise

- Version field (4 bits)
- Priority value (4 bits)
- Flow label (28 bits)
- Length of the "payload" (16 bits)

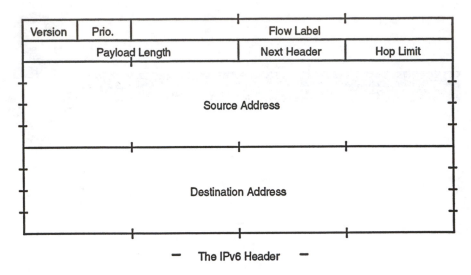

Version	Prio.	Flow Label		
Payload Length			Next Header	Hop Limit
Source Address				
Destination Address				

—   The IPv6 Header   —

■ Type of the next header (8 bits)
■ Hop limit (8 bits)

Assuming that the reader is already somewhat familiar with "IP classic," we will start the analysis of the new IP, IPv6, with a comparison to the previous version.

2.1.1 A Comparison of Two Headers

The new header is in fact much simpler than that of the classic IP. We count only six fields and two addresses, while the old version had 10 fixed header fields, two addresses, and some options.

Version	IHL	Type of Service	Total Length	
Identification		Flags	Fragment Offset	
Time to Live		Protocol	Header Checksum	
Source Address				
Destination Address				
Options			Padding	

—   The IPv4 Header   —

In fact, the only field that kept the same meaning and the same position is the version number, which in both cases is encoded in the very first 4 bits of the header. The original idea was to run IPv4 and IPv6 simultaneously on the same wires, on the same local networks, using the same encapsulations and the same link drivers. The network program would use the initial version field to determine the packet's processing. If the version code is 4 (0100 in binary), it recognizes an IPv4 packet, while if the code is 6 (0110 in binary), it recognizes an IPv6 packet. This idea was in fact abandoned, or at least scaled down. Whenever possible, IPv4 and IPv6 will be demultiplexed at the media layer. For example, IPv6 packets will be carried over Ethernet with the content type 86DD (hexadecimal) instead of IPv4's 8000.

Six fields were suppressed: the header length, the type of service, the identification, the flags, the fragment offset, and the header checksum. Three fields were renamed, and in some cases slightly redefined: the length, the protocol type and the time to live. The option mechanism was entirely revised, and two new fields were added: a priority and a flow label.

2.1.2 Simplifications

The IPv4 header was based on the state of the art of 1975. We should not be surprised to learn that, about 20 years later, we know better. We could thus proceed with three major simplifications:

- Assign a fixed format to all headers
- Remove the header checksum
- Remove the hop-by-hop segmentation procedure

IPv6 headers do not contain any optional element. This does not mean that we cannot express options for special-case packets. But we will see in the next section that this is not achieved with a variable-length *option field* as in IPv4. Instead, *extension headers* are appended after the main header. An obvious consequence is that there is no need in IPv6 for a header length field (IHL).

Removing the header checksum may seem a rather bold move. The main advantage is to diminish the cost of header processing, because there is no need to check and update the checksum at each relay. The obvious risk is that undetected errors may result in misrouted packets. This risk is, however, minimal since most encapsulation procedures include a packet checksum. One finds checksums in the media access control procedures of IEEE-802 networks, in the adaptation layers for ATM circuits, and in the framing procedures of the Point-to-Point Protocol (PPP) for serial links.

IPv4 included a fragmentation procedure so that senders could send large packets without worrying about the capacities of relays. These large packets could be chopped into adequately sized fragments, if needed. The recipients would wait for the arrival of all these segments and reconstitute the packet. But we learned an important lesson from the experience with transport control protocols: the unit of transmission should also be the unit of control. Suppose that we try to transmit large packets over a network that can carry only small segments. The successful transmission of a packet depends on the successful transmission of each segment. If only one is missing, the whole packet should be transmitted again, resulting in a very inefficient usage of the network. The rule with IPv6 is that hosts should learn the maximum acceptable segment size through a procedure called *path MTU discovery*. If they try to send larger packets, these packets will simply be rejected by the network. As a consequence, there is no need in IPv6 for the segmentation control fields of IPv4, that is, the packet Identification, the segmentation control Flags, and the Fragment Offset. IPv6 includes, however, an end to end segmentation procedure, which will be described in the next section. Also, all IPv6 networks are supposed to be able to carry a payload of 536 octets. Hosts that do not want to discover, or remember, the path MTU can simply send small packets.

The last simplification of IPv6 is the removal of the Type Of Service field. In IPv4, hosts would set the TOS to indicate preferences for the wider, shortest, cheapest, or safest paths. However, this field was not frequently set by applications. We will see in Chapter 6 how IPv6 provides mechanisms for handling these preferences.

2.1.3 Classic Parameters, Revised

Just like IPv4, the IPv6 header includes indications of the packet length, the time to live and the protocol type. However, the definitions of these fields were revisited in the light of experience.

The total length of IPv4 is replaced by the *payload length* of IPv6. There is a subtle difference, because the payload length, by definition, is the length of the data carried after the header. Suppose for example that the payload is a TCP packet made of 20 bytes of TCP header and 400 bytes of application data. In IPv4, we would prepend a 20-byte IPv4 header in front of this TCP packet, and the total length would be 440. In IPv6, we will prepend a 40-byte IPv6 header, but the payload length will be set to 420, not 460. In IPv6 as well as IPv4, the length field is encoded on 16 bits, which limits the packet size to 64 kilobytes. We will see later that IPv6 has in fact some provision for larger packets, using the "jumbogram" option.

The protocol type field was renamed *next header* type to reflect the new organization of the IP packets. In IPv4, the IP header is always immediately followed by the transport protocol data, for example an UDP or TCP packet. The simpler of the IPv6 packets will have exactly the same structure, in which case the next header type will be set to the protocol type of UDP (17) or TCP (6). But we will see in the next section that one can also interleave *extension headers* between the IP and TCP or UDP payload. The next header type will then be set to the type of the first extension header.

The renaming of the time to live field to *hop limit* follows a sound design principle, truth in advertising. In IPv4, the time to live was expressed as a number of seconds, indicating how long the packet could remain in the network before being destroyed. The notion of time to live was based on a theoretical analysis of transport control protocols. If packets were allowed to remain infinitely in the network, old copies could pop out at unexpected times and cause protocol errors. TCP, for example, has the notion that a *connection context* shall remain idle for some time after the end of the connection, in order to ensure that all packets belonging to the old instantiation of the context have been purged from the network. This mechanism only works if the transport protocol machinery knows how long a packet can stay in the network, which is indeed the purpose of the TTL field. The IPv4 specification mandates that the TTL be decremented by each router from 1 second or the time spent waiting in the router queues if it is larger than 1 second. But it is very difficult to actually estimate the waiting time of a specific packet. Since this time is usually counted in milliseconds rather than seconds, most routers simply decrement the TTL by 1 at each relay. This behavior has been officialized in IPv6, hence the new name of the field. It counts a number of hops, not a number of seconds. Transport protocols are supposed to provide their own protections against the resurgence of old packets, for example by using time stamps as specified in RFC1323 or large numbering fields.

2.1.4 New Fields

There are two fields in the IPv6 header that were not present in IPv4, the *flow label* and the *priority*. Both are mostly designed to facilitate the handling of real-time traffic. The priority field has 16 possible values. By and large, it plays the same role as the precedence field of IPv4.

The flow label is used to distinguish packets that require the same treatment, that is, they are sent by a given source to a given destination with a given set of options. We will detail the handling of these fields in Chapter 6.

2.2 From Options to Extension Headers

The IPv4 header had room for options, allowing special-case treatment of some packets. The original specification included codes for security options, source routing, and recording or time stamping. Options, however, fell gradually out of use, mostly because of performance effects.

The packet forwarding code is a highly optimized part of the routers' software. Programmers are literally counting the instructions needed to process a packet, because any reduction in this number results in higher performances. The routers that can forward more packets per second than the competition will indeed be more successful in the market. The most common way to speed up the code's performance is to concentrate on the most frequent packets, to let them follow a *fast path* in the program. Packets with options cannot follow the fast path, because by definition they require special treatment. Very often, they will simply be placed in a secondary queue and treated as "second class citizens" by a slower, less optimized piece of software. As a result, application programmers observe that any use of option results in a performance penalty. They tend to use only very simple packets. As optioned packets become less and less frequent, the designers of routers have fewer reasons to process options efficiently. If we pursue this process for several years, we may as well remove the options from the IPv4 specification, because nobody will use any of them.

There are, however, good reasons to require special-case treatment of some packets, for example if one wants to request a specific route through source routing or if one wants to specify a particular handling of the packet by the receiver. Learning from the IPv4 experience, IPv6 specifies how these special-case treatments can be obtained through extension headers.

2.2.1 A Daisy Chain of Headers

In IPv4, the payload, for example, the TCP packet, immediately follows the IP header. In IPv6, it is possible to insert an arbitrary number of *extension headers* between the Internet header and the payload. Each header is identified by a header type and carries the header type of the following header in the chain, or that of the payload in the case of the last extension.

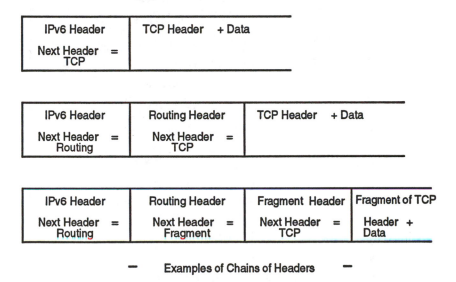

— Examples of Chains of Headers —

The current IPv6 specification defines six extension headers:

- Hop-by-hop options header
- Routing header
- Fragment header
- Authentication header
- Encrypted security payload
- Destination options header

The authentication header and the encrypted payload will be reviewed in Chapter 5. The other extensions will be detailed in the next sections. Each extension is identified by a header type. We observe that the IPv6 next header field may contain either the type of an extension header or the protocol type of the payload, for example, TCP or UDP. In consequence, header types must not conflict with protocol types and are assigned out of the same 256 range of numbers. Most of the types are common to IPv4 and IPv6, although some are slightly different.

Decimal	Keyword	Header Type	
0		Reserved (IPv4)	
	HBH	Hop by hop options (IPv6)	
1	ICMP	Internet Control Message (IPv4)	
2	IGMP	Internet Group Management (IPv4)	
2	ICMP	Internet Control Message (IPv6)	
3	GGP	Gateway-to-Gateway	
4	IP	IP in IP (IPv4 encapsulation)	
5	ST	Stream	
6	TCP	Transmission Control	
17	UDP	User Datagram	
29	ISO-TP4	ISO Transport Protocol Class	4
43	RH	Routing Header (IPv6)	
44	FH	Fragmentation Header (IPv6)	
45	IDRP	Interdomain Routing Protocol	
51	AH	Authentication Header	
52	ESP	Encrypted Security Payload	
59	Null	No next header (IPv6)	
80	ISO-IP	ISO Internet Protocol (CLNP)	
88	IGRP	IGRP	
89	OSPF	Open Shortest Path First	
255		Reserved	
—	Table of Protocol and Header Types		—

2.2.2 Routing Header

The handling of options within IPv6 is best exemplified with the routing header, which plays the same role as the source routing option of IPv4. This header essentially carries a list of intermediate addresses through which the packet shall be relayed, a *source route* that may be either strict or loose.

The routing header is composed of a set of parameters, followed by a list of addresses. The first 32 bits contain four 8-bit integers:

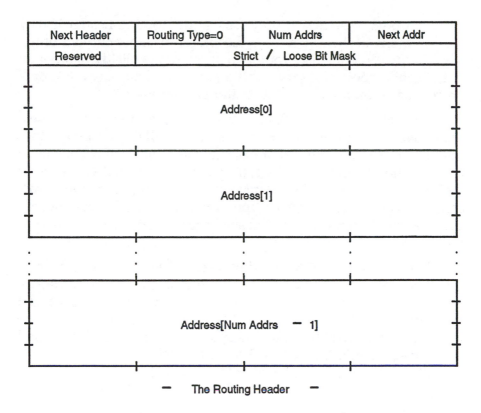

Next Header	Routing Type=0	Num Addrs	Next Addr
Reserved		Strict / Loose Bit Mask	

Address[0]

Address[1]

Address[Num Addrs — 1]

— The Routing Header —

- The *next header*, which identifies the type of header immediately following the routing header in the daisy chain of headers
- The *routing type*, set to 0 according to the current specification; further values would perhaps later be used to identify alternative header formats
- The number of addresses in the list, *Num Addr*; the routing header contains at most 24 addresses
- The number of the next address in the list, *Next Addr*.

The next 32 bits contain a reserved octet, which may be used in future versions of the routing header, and a 24-bit bit mask. The bits in this mask are numbered 0 to 23, left to right. They are used to determine whether the source routing shall be strict or loose.

In IPv4, source routes were encoded in an optional header field that all routers needed to check, even if they were not one of the explicit relays in the source route. As a consequence, the handling of source routed packets was very slow and the option was not used much. In IPv6, routers will only look at the routing header if they recognize one of their own addresses in the destination field of the main header. Intermediate routers that are not explicitly mentioned in the source route will forward the packet without any additional processing. This should result in better performance.

The station that recognizes one of its own addresses in the destination field examines the routing header. It will first check whether the Next Addr value equals or exceeds the number of addresses in the list, Num Addr. If this is true, the packet has arrived at the end of the source route. The station skips over the routing header and processes the next header, whose type is indicated in the next header parameter. Otherwise, the station shall proceed with the source routing.

If the bit numbered Next Addr is set in the strict–loose bit mask, the station shall check that the next value in the list of addresses, *Address[Next Addr]*, is the address of a neighbor. If the bit is set and if the next destination is not that of a neighbor, the packet will be rejected. Otherwise, the station swaps the destination address, and the next element in the address list Address[Next Addr] increments the value of Next Addr and forwards the packet.

2.2.3 Fragment Header

Contrary to IPv4, IPv6 routers do not fragment oversized packets. Everything happens as if the IPv4 *don't fragment* bit was implicitly set. If a packet is larger than the next hop's MTU, it will be rejected and an ICMP message will be sent back. However, there is a provision in IPv6 to fragment packets before they are sent in the network. Suppose that I want to send a 2800-byte payload on my Ethernet interface. I know that the MTU is 1500 bytes. I will thus send two packets of at most 1500 bytes each. In each of these packets, I will insert a *fragment header* between the basic IPv6 header and the payload:

IPv6 header	fragment header 1	First	1400 octets

IPv6 header	fragment header 2	Last	1400 octets

Splitting 2800 Octets into Two Fragments

Each fragment will be routed independently. The fragment header contains sufficient information to enable the destination to concatenate the fragments.

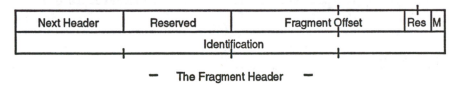

— The Fragment Header —

Apart from the next header parameter, which identifies the next header in the daisy chain, the fields in the IPv6 fragment header are almost identical to the fragmentation control parameters of the IPv4 header. The *identification* is equivalent to the packet identification, with the notable difference that it is encoded on 32 bits instead of 16. The *fragment offset* also plays the same role as the offset field of IPv4, but is encoded slightly differently. IPv4 uses the least significant 13 bits of a 16-bit word, while IPv6 encodes the offset in the most significant bits. In both cases, fragmentation is supposed to occur on a 64-bit word boundary. The IPv4 offset must be multiplied by 8 to obtain an octet offset, while in IPv6 it suffices to zero the three least significant bits. In fact, the main difference lies in the flag fields. There is no fragmentation control bit in the IPv6 header because this header is only inserted when the sender has decided to fragment the packet. We will only find a *more fragment* bit, which will be set to 1 for all but the last fragment of a complete packet.

2.2.4 Destination Options Header

There will be two ways to add functionality to IPv6. The first is to define a new extension header type that will be carried transparently throughout the network and will only be examined by the station specified in the destination address. This first extension method has however two inconveniences:

■ It requires the allocation of header-type numbers. There are only 256 such numbers, and they are used for extension headers as well as payload types, such as UDP, TCP or alternatives. They are a relatively scarce resource that should not be wasted.

■ It requires that both source and destination understand the new option. If a station does not understand the type of a header, it can only reject the whole packet.

The IPv6 *options header* obviates this inconvenience. It uses a single header type (60) to define a generic *destination options* header. This header may contain as a parameter one or several options identified by option types. The specification of the header is minimal.

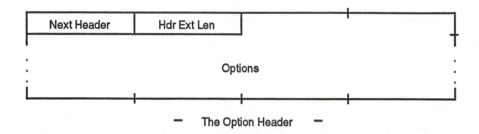

— The Option Header —

The only parameters of the header are the next header type, used in the daisy chaining of headers, and an 8-bit length field. The length field indicates the number of 64-bit words in the options header, not including the first 64 bits. For example, if the option header is composed of exactly 8 octets, the value of the length field will be 0. If the option header is composed of 32 octets, the value of the field will be 3. This seemingly complex convention is typical of a design rule followed by Steve Deering, the main author of the specification. Suppose that we had opted for the classic convention of encoding a length of 1 if the header is 8 octets long, 4 if it is 32 octets long, and so on. We would have to declare illegal the use of a zero-length field, and all implementations would have to test that the length was not null. A test translates into a branch in the program, something that may break the pipelining optimizations of modern RISC processors. With the current convention, the test is replaced by an *increment by 1* operation, which results in a much more streamlined code.

The *options* field contains a list of options. Each option is encoded as a variable number of octets:

Option Type	Opt Data Len	Option Data

The *option type* is the 8-bit identifier of the type of option. It is followed by an 8-bit integer that encodes the number of octets in the option data field. The option type identifiers are structured as

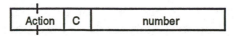

The two high-order bits encode the action that must be taken if the processing node does not recognize the option. The third bit indicates whether the option may change en route. The last bit encodes the option number itself.

Some options merely provide additional information on the packet context or express preferences. If they are not recognized, they can be safely ignored. The processing node will merely skip the option data field, whose length is indicated by the option data length octet, and try to process the remaining options in the header. Some options, on the contrary, are critical and cannot be safely ignored. The packet must be discarded. However, when a station discards a packet, the general rule is to send back an ICMP report. This may or may not be what the sender expects. The action bits are used to specify the requested actions.

Bits	Action
00	Skip over this option
01	Discard the packet, no ICMP report
10	Discard the packet, send ICMP report even if the destination address is multicast
11	Discard the packet, send ICMP report if the destination address is not multicast

— Handling of Unrecognized Options —

When an ICMP report is sent, the code should be set to Parameter Problem (2) and the parameter should point to the unrecognized option type.

The *change en route* bit indicates whether the option may be modified by intermediate relays, similarly to the address list in the routing header. Such options should not be taken into account by end to end checksums.

The options are defined by their option type. These types will be registered by the IANA and documented in specific RFCs. When the option is defined, one will specify its type, its length, and the structure of its internal parameters. One will also specify alignment requirements. For example, if one options parameter is a 32-bit integer, one will ensure that its encoding starts on a 32-bit boundary. The alignment is specified in terms of a period x and an offset y which is noted in a compact form as xn+y. For example, a notation of 2n means that the option may start on any 16-bit boundary, the period being two octets. A notation of 8n+2 means that the option should start two octets after a 64-bit boundary.

Only two options are defined in the current specification, in fact two padding options. The first, Pad1, is composed of a single null byte. By exception to the general rule, this null byte should not be followed by a length octet. One can use any number of null bytes to fill the gap between two options or to fill the option data field to the last 64-bit boundary. If more than one octet shall be skipped, one should, however, use the second padding option, Pad 2 of code 1, whose length field indicates the number of octets that shall be skipped.

2.2.5 Hop-by-Hop Options

The destination option header is a regular extension header, which will only be processed when the packet has reached its final destination. This is in conformance with the general IPv6 philosophy of avoiding unnecessary processing by intermediate relays. However, some management functions, or some debugging functions, require that additional information be passed to all routers. This is the purpose of the hop-by-hop options header. It is identified by the header type 0. A null next header value in the IPv6 header implies the presence of the hop-by-hop option header that shall be processed even if the destination address is not one of the local node addresses.

The hop-by-hop options header has exactly the same format as the destination option header, and hop-by-hop options also have the same encoding rules as the destination options. The padding options Pad1 and PadN can be found in both headers. In addition, the current specification also defines a *jumbo payload* option, with option type 194.

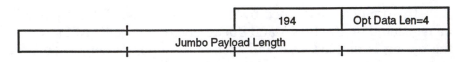

This option is used to send very large packets whose length could not be encoded on 16 bits only. When this option is used, the

IPv6 length field is set to zero. The processing node shall decode the jumbo payload option to find out the actual packet length, encoded as a 32-bit integer. To facilitate the processing of this length field, the alignment requirement of option 194 is set to 4n + 2 so that the length field itself starts on a 32-bit boundary.

The jumbo payload option shall not be used if the length is less than 65,535 octets. It shall also not be used if the packet carries a fragment header. In fact, the definition of the jumbo payload option is a compromise between the initial design of IPv6 and the networking requirements of supercomputers. This is one controversial aspect of the IPv6 design which we will develop it in Section 2.6.

2.2.6 Extension Header Order

A packet may well contain more than one extension header. This should not pose any problem to the receiving nodes, which will simply process the headers in the order in which they are received. The early design documents described this as an "onion-peeling" procedure. Each successive layer would be processed in turn, just like removing each layer of an onion in turn. Indeed, some of the layers have a magic of their own, like the fragment layer or the routing layer, or rather the routing header and fragment header. Fragmented packets must be reassembled before any further processing. It is only after the last fragment has arrived that the node can start unpeeling the next header. The routing header is a different case. If a node is not the last in the list of intermediate relays, it should update the destination field and forward the packet, without even looking into the next header.

The processing order is determined by the order of the headers in the daisy chain. This order is specified by the initial sender. The IPv6 specifications include a recommended order:

1. *IPv6 header*

2. *Hop-by-hop options header*

3. *Destination options header (1)*

4. *Routing header*

5. *Fragment header*

6. *Authentication header*

7. *Destination options header (2)*

8. *Upper-layer header (for example, TCP or UDP)*

Each of these headers is indeed optional. There is no need to insert a hop-by-hop header if one does not use hop-by-hop options. One will not use the routing header if one does not want to mandate a specific routing. One will not use any fragmentation header if the packet is smaller than the path's MTU. The recommended order is in fact a ranking of headers; it provides guidelines for implementors. We may observe that the destination option header is listed twice. If we want specify tunneling options that will be processed by all intermediate relays, we will place these options before the routing header. If, on the other hand, we want to pass information to the final destination, we will insert the option header immediately before the upper-layer header.

If we want to mandate only one relay in the path, we may replace the routing header by a complete IPv6 packet in order to build up a tunnel. The header type for the encapsulation of IPv6 is 41. This encapsulated payload will have the same recommended ordering as the routing header. The processing of the header will be somewhat faster, because all data that precede the encapsulation are simply removed.

There may be some need (e.g., for debugging purposes) to send a packet that does not include any upper-layer data. In this case, the daisy chain of headers should be ended by a *no next header* type, whose value is 59.

2.3 The Evolution of ICMP

The Internet Control Message Protocol (ICMP) was also revised during the definition of IPv6. The revision followed the same guidelines as that of the Internet Protocol itself. The protocol was streamlined. Some functionalities that were present in the IPv4 ICMP, but were not used anymore, have been removed. Then the protocol was made more complete by incorporating the multicast control functions of the IPv4 Group Membership protocol, IGMP. Some formats were extended to carry the larger fields of IPv6. As a result, the new ICMP is not compatible with the old one. To avoid confusion, it is identified by a different header type, 2 instead of 1. The type 2 was in fact used for the IPv4 IGMP.

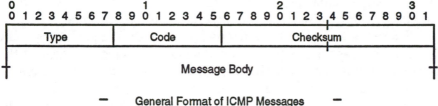

<table>
<tr><td>0</td><td>1</td><td>2</td><td>3</td></tr>
</table>

```
 0                   1                   2                   3
 0 1 2 3 4 5 6 7 8 9 0 1 2 3 4 5 6 7 8 9 0 1 2 3 4 5 6 7 8 9 0 1
+-----------------+-----------------+-------------------------------+
|      Type       |      Code       |           Checksum            |
+-----------------+-----------------+-------------------------------+
|                         Message Body                             |
+                                                                  +
```

—   General Format of ICMP Messages   —

All IPv6 ICMP messages have the same general format, comprising a type, a code, a checksum, and a variable-length body. The checksum is computed according to the general IPv6 rules, which will be described later. It covers both the ICMP packet itself and the fixed fields of the IPv6 header. The precise format of the message body, as well as the different values of the code parameter, depend on the ICMP type. The IPv6 specifications currently define 14 different types.

1	Destination Unreachable
2	Packet Too Big
3	Time Exceeded
4	Parameter Problem
128	Echo Request
129	Echo Reply
130	Group Membership Query
131	Group Membership Report
132	Group Membership Termination
133	Router Solicitation
134	Router Advertisement
135	Neighbor Solicitation
136	Neighbor Advertisement
137	Redirect

—   Currently Defined ICMP Types   —

Codes 1 to 4 describe error messages. Codes 133, 134, 135, 136, and 137 are used by the neighbor discovery and autoconfiguration procedures, described in Chapter 4. Codes 128 and 129 define the IPv6 equivalent of the ping function. Codes 130 to 132 are used in the group membership procedures, which we will describe in Chapter 3.

2.3.1 Error Messages

Whenever an IPv6 node discards a packet, it may send an ICMP error report to the original destination. The nodes should not, however, send error reports in response to multicast packets, because this could create avalanches, nor in response to ICMP packets, because this could create infinite loops of erroneous ICMP packets.

There are four possible reasons for discarding a packet. Specific ICMP types describe whether the packet was rejected because the destination is unreachable, because the packet is too big, because it has exceeded its time to live, or because of a parameter problem. All error messages have similar formats. The 64-bit header contains the ICMP type, a code, and a 32-bit parameter. The remainder of the ICMP packet contains a copy of the original packet. If the original packet is too large to fit entirely in a 576-octet message, it will be truncated.

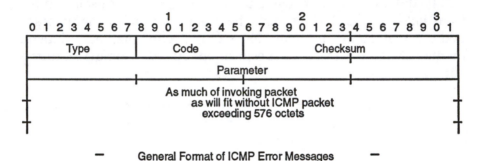

General Format of ICMP Error Messages

The meaning of code and parameter depend on the ICMP type. In the case of the *destination unreachable message,* the type is set to 1, the parameter field is not used and should be left at zero, and the code field can take one of four values:

0   **No route to destination**

1   **Communication with destination administratively prohibited**

3   **Address unreachable**

4   **Port unreachable**

Code 0 should be used when the router does not know any path toward the final destination. Code 1 will typically be used by a "firewall" that restricts the possibility of sending packets in or out of a given network in an attempt to achieve some degree of security. Code 3 will be used when the packet almost reached the final destination but could not be delivered, for example, when the final router could not resolve the IPv6 address into a link layer address.

In the case of the *packet too big message,* the type is set to 2, the code field is not used and should be left to zero, and the parameter field contains the maximum transmission unit (MTU) of the next-hop link. These messages allow hosts to efficiently implement the *MTU discovery* procedure. They start by sending a large packet, as large as the local interface allows. If this is too large for some link in the path, they will receive a packet too big message and be given the MTU of the next-hop link. The link can immediately try using this new value. If another downstream link is even more constrained, they will receive another error message and will have to try again, using the MTU of this more constrained link. Experience shows that, in practice, the algorithm rapidly converges toward an acceptable value. By exception to the general rule, the packet too big messages can also be sent in response to a packet destined to an IPv6 multicast address. This will allow Path MTU discovery to work for IPv6 multicast.

In the case of the *time exceeded message*, the type is set to 3, the parameter field is not used and should be left at zero, and the code field can take one of two values:

0 **Hop limit exceeded in transit**

1 **Fragment reassembly time exceeded**

The hop limit exceeded message will be sent when a packet is discarded in transit. When an IPv6 packet is sent as a collection of fragments, using the fragment header, the *fragment reassembly* problem will occur if a fragment is lost. IPv6 nodes will start a timer whenever they start reassembling a packet. The timer should range between 1 and 2 minutes. A packet loss is detected if this timer elapses before the last segment arrives.

A *parameter problem* is detected when the receiving node cannot process an incoming packet. The ICMP type will be set to 4 and the parameter will contain a *pointer* that identifies the octet offset within the incoming packet where the problem was detected. There are three possible code values:

0 **Erroneous header field**

1 **Unrecognized next header type**

2 **Unrecognized IPv6 option**

In the case of long daisy chains of headers, the pointer may have a large value, pointing in fact toward a fraction of the incoming packet that could not be copied in the ICMP report.

2.3.2 The IPv6 Ping

The echo request and echo reply messages have the same format. When an IPv6 node wants to trigger an echo from a remote node, it sends an *echo request*. The type field shall be set to 128, and the code shall be set to 0. The node may choose an identifier value in order to help to match replies with requests. If it sends several successive requests to the same destination, it will assign them successive sequence numbers.

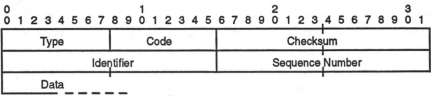

—   ICMP Echo Messages in IPv6   —

The *echo reply* will be sent to the source address of the incoming packet. The ICMP echo reply message will be almost identical to the incoming message. The only differences will be the type field, which will be set to 129, and the checksum field, which will be recomputed.

2.4 Impact on the Upper Layers

Changing the Internet Protocol has some impact on the upper layers. This impact is minimal, because the IPv6 datagram service is identical to the classical IP service. However, the implementation of transport protocols such as TCP or UDP will have to be updated to take into account the larger addresses and the new format of the ICMP messages. The specifications of these protocols will have to be updated in at least one regard, the need to take into account the new addresses when computing the transport-level checksums.

The new definition of addresses also has an impact on the applications themselves. The name service will have to return long IPv6 addresses that the applications will have to pass to the transport protocols through the programming interface.

2.4.1 Upper-layer Checksums

Transport protocols such as TCP or UDP attach a checksum to their packets. The goal of this checksum is to detect transmission errors, bits or bytes that would be altered either during their transmission on a link or within a router's memory. The checksum is computed over an imaginary packet, which is the concatenation of the transport packet that is actually transmitted and a pseudoheader.

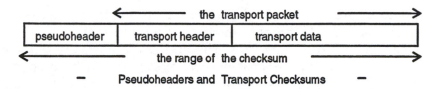

Pseudoheaders and Transport Checksums

The *pseudoheader* is a representation of a nominal Internet Protocol header. By including both the source and the destination address in the checksum, one can detect misdelivery. If for some reason the destination or the source address is altered in transit, the value of the pseudoheader will not match the initial value, and the checksum verification will fail.

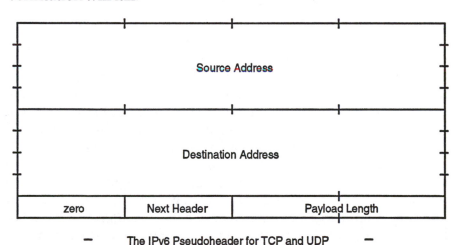

The IPv6 Pseudoheader for TCP and UDP

The definition of the pseudoheader is an integral part of the TCP or UDP specification and, in fact, of any upper-layer protocol that includes addresses in its checksum computation. This part should be updated in order to reflect the change in the address size. A new version of the TCP and UDP pseudoheader is provided in the

IPv6 specification. It includes the source and destination address, the next header type, and the payload length.

A difference from IPv4 is that IPv6 does not contain any header checksum. In consequence, the use of a checksum at the upper layer is mandatory, even in the case of UDP.

2.4.2 IPv6 in the Domain Name Service

Application programs should normally manipulate domain names such as *sophia.inria.fr*, rather than numeric addresses such as 10.0.0.1 or 1a03:9:2b:3c:5:7ec3:de09:5b73. The address is normally obtained through a lookup in the *domain name service*, the distributed data base that stores various resource records for each Internet domain. These resource records are identified by a type, which is designated by a literal acronym in the documentation and by a type number in the DNS query and response packets.

The IPv4 addresses are stored in records of type A (code 1). Each A record contains one 32-bit address. A new resource record has been defined for IPv6. Because it contains one 128-bit address, and as such is four times larger than the A record, its type has been set to AAAA (code 28).

The DNS data bases also contain a numerical hierarchy that is used for retrieving the name of the host when the address is available. One can derive from IPv4 addresses a domain name by reversing the order of the components and appending the domain name "in-addr.arpa." For example, the IPv4 address 123.45.67.89 will be represented as 89.67.45.123.in-addr.arpa. Servers use this reverse name to retrieve the real domain name associated with an address. A similar service is defined for IPv6. The problem was that IPv6 addresses do not have natural boundaries. The separations between provider and subscriber, network and subnetwork, and subnetwork and host identifier do not have to fall on a 32-bit, 16-bit or even 8-bit boundary. The numeric names are thus built by first representing the address as a sequence of hexadecimal digits, or nibbles, then reversing their order, separating them by dots, and appending the suffix .IP6.INT. According to these rules, an IPv6 address such as 4321:0:1:2:3:4:567:89ab will be represented in the domain name system as

b.a.9.8.7.6.5.0.4.0.0.0.3.0.0.0.2.0.0.0.1.0.0.0.0.0.0.0.1.2.3.4.IP6.INT.

The choice of an international domain, rather than the .arpa domain of IPv4, is supposed to reflect the international nature of the Internet.

2.4.3 Programming Interface

The definition of a standard programming interface for IPv6 will facilitate the upgrading of existing applications. It will also make it easy for programmers to use the new facilities provided by IPv6. Because IPv6 is very similar to IPv4, the core socket functions such as accept, connect, or send remain unchanged. The differences between IPv6 and IPv4 are located in three types of interfaces:

■ Address data structures

■ Name-to-address translation functions

■ Address conversion functions

A new address family, AF_INET6, and a new protocol family, PF_INET6, were added to the regular socket library. Addresses of the AF_INET6 family will be represented by the *in_addr6* structure:

```
struct in_addr6    {
            u_long s6_addr[4];          /  * IPv6 address    * /
}
```

The IPv4 address data structure, sockaddr_in, does not provide enough space for holding this structure. It is replaced by the new *sockaddr_in6* structure, or rather by two structures, one for 4.3 BSD systems and another, which includes a length field, for 4.4 BSD systems; a programming flag can be used to trigger conditional compilation. The structures include a flow label as well as the transport port number and the IPv6 address. Socket addresses must always be cast as generic *sockaddr* structures when used as arguments to system calls of the socket library

```
struct sockaddr_in6     {
            u_short             sin6_family;         /*  AF_INET6  */
            u_short             sin6_port;           /*  Transport layer port     , /  # */
            u_long              sin6-_lowlabel;      /*  IPv6 flow label      */
            struct        in_addr6 sin6_addr;        /*  IPv6 address     * /
};
                    ─      IPv6 Socket Address Structure for 4.3 BSD        ─
```

```
#define SIN6_LEN

struct sockaddr_in6      {
            u_char                sin6_len;           /*  length of this struct        */
            u_char                sin6_family;        /*  AF_INET6  */
            u_short               sin6_port;          /*  Transport layer port        # */
            u_long                sin6_flowlabel;     /*  IPv6 flow label        */
            struct        in_addr6 sin6_addr;         /*  IPv6 address        */
},
```

—   IPv6 Socket Address Structure for 4.4 BSD   —

The IPv4 address translation functions *gethostbyname* and *gethostbyaddr* will be replaced by two new functions, *hostname2addr* and *addr2hostname*. The new functions allow the programmer to specify the type of addresses that the application expects, either AF_INET or AF_INET6. The *host entry* structure was already designed to handle multiple address types. It will not be changed.

The conversion between the ASCII and network forms of IPv4 addresses is currently performed by two IPv4 specific functions, *inet_ntoa* and *inet_addr*. These functions are replaced by the new generic procedures *ascii2addr* and *addr2ascii* that take an additional argument, the address family.

In the process of designing the IPv6 API, the authors of the specification performed a rather exhaustive test. They took many existing applications and tried to port them to the new interface. The overall result is rather encouraging: in many cases, the upgrade is a simple and straightforward process. However, they encountered a few problems that were treated by adding special functions to the programming interface.

The authors observed that the handling of addresses by applications can be greatly simplified if both IPv4 and IPv6 addresses are represented in a single format. The API defines an IPv4 prefix, 0:0:0:0:0:FFFF. IPv4 addresses can be represented in IPv6 format by concatenating this 96-bit prefix and the 32-bit address value. IPv4 aware implementations, if they want to make special decisions, can test the prefix through the is_ipv4_addr function call.

Some applications are divided into two separate programs, a listener that accepts connections and a processor that is launched by the listener, using an *exec* system call. The connection is passed as a system parameter in UNIX, a file descriptor. Problems arise if the processor is not upgraded at the same time as the listener, because one expects a socket of type IPv4, while the other passes an IPv6 socket. The authors added a specific system call, a new *setsockopt* option, that listeners can use to transform a PF_INET6 socket into a PF_INET socket, and vice versa, before passing that socket to the processor program.

New setsockopt options have also been defined for retrieving the source routes of incoming packets, for positioning the source routes of outgoing packets, for handling the IPv6 hop limit, and for handling multicast groups.

2.5 Points of Controversy

The choice of the details of the IPv6 specifications were indeed not exempt from controversies. Most of the debates were related to the choice of the 128-bit address size. We will present these in Chapter 3. But the choice of an 8-bit hop count and a 16-bit length field, the absence of a checksum, and the structure of the source routing header also generated some discussion.

2.5.1 Do We Need More Than 255 Hops?

As the Internet grows larger and larger, we may expect that the average number of relays between two points will also increase. Some participants to the discussion felt that allowing only 8 bits for the encoding to the hop count was very shortsighted. Connections that require more than 32 hops already exist. What if someday the Internet grows so large that we need more than 255 hops? Why not cut the risk and use a 16-bit hop count?

Steve Deering resisted firmly. In fact, this would not be the sole occasion where Steve demonstrated his ability to stubbornly resist what he perceived as gratuitous changes. What is true of the hop count could in fact be said of any other field. We would feel more comfortable if the flow label were 64 bit, if the payload type were 16 bit, if the length field were 32 bit, if we had included this or that extra option in the header. But, then, the header would be so bloated and the overhead so large that performance would suffer. Before accepting an increase to the length of any field, we should first look deeply at the consequences.

Raising the size of the hop count was rejected because having a very large number of relays between two nodes is undesirable in the first place and also because, if we allowed such a large number of relays, the hop count would be useless.

The main function of the hop count is to make sure that the mis-routed packet is eventually discarded, rather than looping an infinite amount of time in the network. By recycling the old traffic on the same links again and again, routing loops act as load multipliers. If a packet hop count is set to some small value such as 32 or even 64, we guarantee that, even in the case of loops, it will show up only 32 or 64 times on Internet links. But if we allow the hop count to be very large, for example 32,000 or 64,000, then looping packets will be allowed to be relayed that many times before being discarded. The hop count is a kind of safety net for routing procedures, but a very large hop count would be a very loose safety net.

Each relay contributes to some transit delay and some delay variance. Having very many relays would mean an Internet with very poor response times, quite inadequate for the new multimedia applications. There is probably no need to have several hundred hops even in a large Internet. The routing structure should have some degree of hierarchy so that main trunks cross continents or oceans without being explicitly relayed from city to city or island to island. Having a relatively small hop count is thus a good thing, because it will force managers to correctly architect their network and avoid unnecessary relaying.

2.5.2 Should Packets Be Larger Than 64K?

The size of the length field was as much discussed as that of the hop count, if not more. Some high-speed networks already allow the transmission of very large packets, much larger than the meager 64 kilobytes that could be encoded in 16 bits.

Steve Deering again provided stern resistance to the suggestion that we increase the size of the length field. He pointed out that chopping very large packets in slices of 64K only resulted in an over-head of about 0.06%, that is, 40 octets per 64K packet. Then he argued that IPv6 is an internetworking protocol, that IPv6 packets will have to be relayed by Internet routers, and that allowing very large packets is very inefficient in this environment, because it can increase the size of queues and the variability of queuing delays. The very large packets option was in fact pushed by some users and makers of supercomputers. Supercomputers do not like being inter-rupted, and prefer to transfer very large segments of memory.

In the end, a compromise was found in the form of the *jumbo-gram* option. Packets larger than 64K can be sent, if the media and the partner allow, by leaving the length field null in the main header and coding the actual length as a 32-bit integer in the jumbogram option field. This solution would be unacceptable if most packets were expected to be larger than 64K, because hop by hop options are very hard to process by routers. But it is acceptable by supercomputers, because their very large memory pages are generally exchanged over direct connections.

2.5.3 Can We Live without a Checksum?

The absence of checksum in IPv6 was a rather bold move. Some felt that it was not unlike removing a car's brakes. The car is lighter and runs faster, but what if errors occur?

In fact, the IPv4 header checksum only provided a very limited amount of safety. It is designed to catch the transmission errors that affect the header but would not be detected by the media-level procedures. In practice, undetected errors do not occur on transmission lines, where the Ethernet or PPP checksums are quite effective, but within the routers themselves. They can be caused by faulty memory boards or by programming errors. But routers have to update the headers, if only to decrement the hop count. They will thus recompute the checksum before sending the packet, hiding their programming errors.

The cost of this limited safety was quite important, involving several instructions within the most critical programming loops. How many packets a router switches per second depends on that loop. Some IPv4 routers already started to cut corners by not verifying incoming checksums, so as to gain an advantage over the competition.

By removing the checksum altogether, we offer to all routers the possibility to achieve better performances. The risk is in fact quite small:

- Changing the version field would cause the packet to be discarded.
- Changing the flowlabel would cause the packet to be routed with the wrong priority.
- Changing the length field to a larger value would probably cause the packet to be discarded because the new length would not be consistent with media-level indications. A change to a lower value would be detected by the end-to-end checksum.

- Changing the payload type would normally cause the packet to be delivered to the right destination and then be rejected by that destination.
- Changing the hop count to a larger value would only cause a problem if the packet were caught in a routing loop. A change to a lower value may cause the packet to be discarded.
- Changing the source address would be detected by the end-to-end checksum, if the source address was included in the pseudoheader.
- Changing the destination address would normally result in an invalid address, causing the packet to be discarded. It might result in a misdelivery that end-to-end checksums would detect.

In fact, these errors could only pose a serious problem if they were systematically caused by a programming error in an intermediate router. But these are precisely the type of errors that the routers are good at hiding in IPv4, because they recompute the header checksum at each hop. On the other hand, systematic errors are easily detected by management procedures.

2.5.4 What Should Be the Structure of the Routing Header?

The Source Demand Routing working group of the IETF has worked for several years to define the Source Demand Routing Protocol (SDRP). This protocol is designed to provide policy route between Internet routing domains. It uses source routing and its packet format is very similar to the routing header extension, so similar that there was an attempt to unify the two designs. But SDRP has a number of specificities:

- To gain performances the successive SDRP addresses are simply copied into the destination header at each relay, not swapped. This means that if there are N relays, the SDRP lists contain $N + 1$ addresses instead of N for the routing header.
- To avoid overhead, some versions of SDRP include a virtual circuit setup procedure so that the full list of relays does not have to be carried in every packet.
- SDRP also includes many more policy controls than the routing header, making it much more complex.

In fact, SDRP is so complex that it is not yet entirely defined. Rather than wait for this definition, Steve Deering and Ross Callon decided to simply move forward with a simple definition for the routing header, to provide the service of IPv4 source routing rather than the policy routes of SDRP. The compromise was to include a version field in the header, or rather a routing type field. The IPv6 specification defines version 0. The SDR working group will probably define another version.

2.6 Further Reading

IPv6 is defined in the "Internet Protocol, Version 6 (IPv6) Specification" by Steve Deering and Robert Hinden. The "Internet Control Message Protocol (ICMPv6) for the Internet Protocol Version 6 (IPv6) Specification" by Steve Deering and Alex Conta defines the IPv6 ICMP. The "DNS Extensions to Support IP version 6" have been specified by Susan Thomson and myself. Robert E. Gilligan, Susan Thomson, and Jim Bound define the BSD API in "IPv6 Program Interfaces for BSD Systems." All these documents should soon be published as RFCs.

The size of the hop count, the size of the length field, and the omission of the checksum were first debated on the SIP working group's list. The same debates were then repeated numerous times in the SIPP and IPv6 lists. The lists archives are available on the Internet.

Routing and Addressing

The most salient feature of IPv6 is the enlarged address format. Going from 32 to 128 bits not only guarantees that we will be able to number thousands of billions of hosts, but it also provides room to insert many more degrees of hierarchy than the basic three layers of network, subnet, and host of IPv4.

3.1 Address Architecture

Since IPv6 is based on the same architecture principle as the classic Internet protocol, IPv4, one could very well expect the IPv6 address to be larger versions of the IPv4 addresses, and one would be basically right. Like IPv4 addresses, IPv6 addresses identify an interface connected to a subnetwork, not a station. As in IPv4, a station that is *multihomed* will have as many addresses as interfaces. In fact, one big difference with IPv4 is that IPv6 routinely allows each interface to be identified by several addresses, in order to facilitate routing or management.

The IPv6 addresses belong to one of three categories:

- Unicast
- Multicast
- Anycast

Unicast is a new name for what we used to call point to point addresses. These addresses identify exactly one interface. More precisely, they identify exactly one interface within their scope of validity. A packet sent to an unicast address will normally be delivered to that interface.

A multicast address identifies a group of stations, or more precisely a group of interfaces. A packet sent toward a multicast address will normally be delivered to all the members of the group.

An anycast address also identifies a group of stations. The difference between multicast and anycast is in the transmission process. Instead of being delivered to all members of the group, packets sent to a unicast address are normally delivered to only one point, the nearest member of the group. This facility did not exist in IPv4, although some researchers, notably Craig Partridge, conducted limited scope experiments and demonstrated its feasibility.

In this section, we will present the notation of IPv6 addresses and the initial definitions of address formats.

3.1.1 Notation of IPv6 Addresses

An IPv6 address is composed of 128 bits. The designers of the protocol chose to write these 128 bits as eight 16-bit integers separated by colons. Each integer is represented by four hexadecimal digits, as in:

FEDC:BA98:7654:3210:FEDC:BA98:7654:3210

Hexadecimal notation has the advantage of being relatively compact and straightforward. It is, however, a bit difficult to manipulate. Some see this lack of user friendliness as a definitive advantage. Users, they say, should manipulate names, not addresses. But then system managers do have to manipulate these addresses. They will have to type them into directory files or administrative data bases. One way to make their life a little bit easier is to allow some abbreviations. Let's start by observing that, at least in the initial stage, we will not be using all 128 bits. There very likely will be many zeros, as in

1080:0000:0000:0000:0008:0800:200C:417A

A first improvement is the authorization to skip leading zeros in each hexadecimal component, that is, writing 0 instead of 0000, 8 instead of 0008, 800 instead of 0800. This leaves us with the reduced form:

1080:0:0:0:8:800:200C:417A

Then the specification introduces yet another simplification, the double-colon convention. Inside an address, a set of consecutive null 16-bit numbers can be replaced by two colons. For example, we can replace three consecutive null numbers in the previous example and obtain the short form:

1080::8:800:200C:417A

Expanding the abbreviation is quite simple. Align whatever is at the left of the double colon to the left of the address: these are the leading 16-bit words. Then align whatever is at the right of the colons to the right of the address and fill up with zeros. The following are valid short forms and their extended notations:

FEDC:BA98::7654:3210, FEDC:BA98:0:0:0:0:7654:3210

FEDC:BA98:7654:3210::, FEDC:BA98:7654:3210:0:0:0:0

::FEDC:BA98:7654:3210, 0:0:0:0:FEDC:BA98:7654:3210

The double-colon convention can only be used once inside an address. For example, the address 0:0:0:BA98:7654:0:0:0 could be abbreviated as ::BA98:7654:0:0:0 or 0:0:0:BA98:7654::, but certainly not as ::BA98:7654::, which would be ambiguous.

Some IPv6 addresses are obtained by prepending 96 zero bits to an IPv4 address. To reduce the risk of erroneous transposition between the dot-decimal notation of IPv4 and the colon-decimal notation of IPv6, the specification introduces a specific format for these addresses. Instead of writing

0:0:0:0:0:0:A00:1

one can leave the last 32 bits in dot decimal form, as in

::10.0.0.1

The specification does not yet introduce a notation for prefixes, that is, the high-order bits of the addresses used by routing protocols. In this book, we will use a notation derived from IPv4, a regular IPv6 address followed by a slash and a number of bits. For example, the notation

FEDC:BA98:7600::/40

describes a 40-bit-long prefix whose binary value is

1111111011011100101110101001100001110110

3.1.2 Initial Assignment

The IPv6 designers know one thing for sure: what they do today will have to be revisited at some point in the future. This is obviously true of option and parameters, but is even more true of address assignment. We are by no means certain that, in 1995, we know the best way to assign addresses. IPv6 implementations are not supposed to have full knowledge of the various address allocation prefixes and formats. In most cases, it is perfectly legitimate for a host to treat addresses as opaque strings of 128 bits. Similarly, the entries in the router tables will be simple prefixes, whose length will vary from 1 to 128 bits. The only exception concerns the *special* addresses. Hosts and routers must indeed recognize multicast addresses, which cannot be processed the same way as unicast or anycast addresses. They must also recognize special addresses, notably the *loopback* addresses and the *site local* and *link local* addresses. The initial addressing architecture defines these prefixes, as well as a prefix for the *provider-based* addresses that will be used during the initial deployment. The architecture document also reserves prefixes for geographic addresses, NSAP-compatible addresses, and IPX-compatible addresses.

Allocation	Prefix (binary)		Fraction of Address Space
Reserved	0000	0000	1/256
Unassigned	0000	0001	1/256
Reserved for NSAP allocation	0000	001	1/128
Reserved for IPX allocation	0000	010	1/128
Unassigned	0000	011	1/128
Unassigned	0000	1	1/32
Unassigned	0001		1/16
Unassigned	001		1/8
Provider-based unicast address	010		1/8
Unassigned	011		1/8
Reserved for geographic- based unicast addresses	100		1/8
Unassigned	101		1/8
Unassigned	110		1/8
Unassigned	1110		1/16
Unassigned	1111	0	1/32
Unassigned	1111	10	1/64
Unassigned	1111	110	1/128
Unassigned	1111	1110 0	1/512
Link local use addresses	1111	1110 10	1/1024
Site local use addresses	1111	1110 11	1/1024
Multicast addresses	1111	1111	1/256

— Initial Address Allocation within IPv6 —

The third column of the table of initial address allocations shows the fraction of the address space that is committed to any given usage. The most significant share is that of provider-based addresses, but this covers only one eighth of the total space. Another equivalent fraction is reserved for geographical addresses, although there is no current plan to use it. All in all, more than 70% of the space remains unassigned, which should provide ample opportunities for trying new assignments in future years.

3.1.3 Provider Addresses

The first IPv6 addresses will be allocated according to a provider-based plan. *Provider-based addresses* are composed of the 3-bit prefix 010 followed by five components. According to the IPv6 addressing architecture, all these components have a variable length.

3	n bits	m bits	o bits	p bits	125-m-n o-p bits
010	registry ID	provider ID	subscriber ID	subnetwork ID	interface ID

— Generic Format of Provider Addresses —

The first component is the *registry*. There are currently three main registries in charge of allocating IPv4 addresses. It is expected that these same registries will also handle IPv6 addresses. The main registry, in charge of North America, is the Internet NIC (Network Information Center), which is operated by NSI under a contract with the U.S. National Science Foundation. The European registry is the NCC (Network Coordination Center) of RIPE, the association of European networks. The APNIC allocates addresses for networks in Asian and Pacific countries. The current plan is to use a 5-bit registry ID, with the following values:

10000 **multiregional (IANA)**

01000 **RIPE NCC**

11000 **INTERNIC**

10100 **APNIC**

Internet service providers are expected to obtain a *provider ID* from these registries. According the initial address allocation plan, the provider ID is a 16-bit number. The 8 following bits will be left to zero in the initial phase. They are reserved for future extensions.

In the current structure, the main registries are supplemented by a large number of national or regional registries, for example, the French NIC managed by INRIA for French networks. These registries will not be identified by a registry number. Instead, they will receive ranges of provider identifiers from the main registries.

Subscribers will receive their addresses from their providers. According the initial address allocation plan, the subscriber ID occupies 24-bit. Providers may indeed structure this field to reflect the internal organization of their networks. The 8 following bits will be left to zero in the initial phase. They are reserved for future extensions. The remaining 64 bits will probably be split into 16 bits for the identification of the *subnetwork* and 48 bits for the identification of the station.

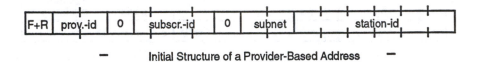

Initial Structure of a Provider-Based Address

Large customers may perhaps obtain shorter identifiers, which will give them the possibility to add one layer of hierarchy on top of the subnetwork. In fact, these large customers may also request to be treated as "their own provider" and obtain a particular form of provider identifier from the local registry.

3.1.4 Special Address Formats

In addition to provider-based addresses, we may expect to encounter five more kinds of unicast addresses:

- Unspecified address
- Loopback addresses
- IPv4-based addresses
- Site local addresses
- Link local addresses

The *unspecified address* is composed of 16 null bytes. It could be noted simply as two colons, the shortcut for 0:0:0:0:0:0:0:0. This address can only be used as a source address by a station that has not yet been configured with a regular address. It can also be used in some control messages when the presence of an address is semantically required but no address is available. It shall never be used as a destination address.

The loopback address *0:0:0:0:0:0:0:1* may be used by a node to send an IPv6 datagram to itself. The loopback address and the unspecified address may never be assigned to an interface.

It is possible to construct IPv6 addresses by prepending a null prefix, made of 96 zero bits, to the 32-bit *IPv4 address*. These addresses will typically be noted by combining the double-colon and the dotted decimal notation of IPv4, as in ::10.0.0.1. They will be used during the transition period, as we will explain in Chapter 7. We should note that the reserved prefix of eight zero bits is common to the unspecified address, the loopback address, and IPv4-derived addresses.

Many organizations use the TCP-IP technology without being actually connected to the Internet, either because they are afraid of the security implications of a direct connection or because they want to set up and try their internal network without waiting to complete the connection procedure. The *site local* addressing prefix, 1111 1110 11, has been reserved for these organizations. A typical site local address will consist of this prefix, a set of zeros, the subnet identifier and the station identifier:

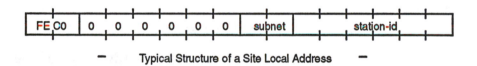

— Typical Structure of a Site Local Address —

The site local addresses cannot be routed on the global Internet. Their unicity is only guaranteed within a site. They can only be used for exchanges between two stations within a single site.

Stations that are not yet configured with either a provider-based address or a site local address may use the *link local addresses*. These addresses are composed of the link local prefix, 1111 1110 10, a set of zeros, and a station identifier:

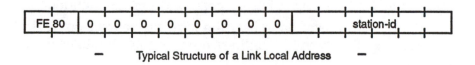

— Typical Structure of a Link Local Address —

These addresses are only defined within a link and can only be used by stations connected to the same link or to the same local network. Packets sent to these addresses will never be relayed by a router. We will see in Chapter 4 how these addresses are used during the phases of configuration.

3.2 Multicasting and Anycasting

Multicasting capabilities were formally added to IPv4 in 1988, with the definition of class D addresses and the Internet Group Management Protocol. The deployment of these capabilities was sped up by the arrival of the MBONE in 1992, but this deployment is still very far from being universal. The designers of IPv6 wanted to take advantage of the deployment of a new protocol to make sure that multicasting is available on all IPv6 nodes. They defined a multicast address format that all routers should recognize, they incorporated the functions of IPv4's IGMP in the basic ICMP protocol of IPv6, and they made sure that all routers could route multicast packets.

The anycasting capabilities of IPv4 were even less advanced. Their incorporation in IPv6 will offer a lot of flexibility to network managers.

3.2.1 Structure of Multicast Addresses

The design of the IPv6 multicast address takes advantage of the experience gained on research networks such as Dartnet since 1988 and also on the MBONE since 1992. Multicast addresses have the following format:

8	4	4	112 bits
11111111	flgs	scop	group ID

The first octet of the address is the multicast prefix 11111111. It is followed by 4 bits of flags, 4 bits of scope, and a group identifier.

Out of the 4 bits of flags, only the fourth is defined in the IPv6 specifications. The three other bits are reserved and should be initialized to zero:

0	0	0	T

The fourth bit is abbreviated T for Transient. A permanently assigned address is a well-known address, assigned by a global Internet numbering authority. A transient address is one that is not permanently assigned. This is what is typically in use in the MBONE today. When a group decides to conduct a multicasting session, it asks the *session directory* tool to pick an address at random. The unicity of this random address is verified by a collision detection algorithm. Once the session is terminated, the address is released.

The scope is encoded as a 4-bit integer. It is used to limit the scope of the multicast group, for example to ensure that packets sent into a local videoconference do not leak on the worldwide Internet. The values are

```
0   reserved
1   node local scope
2   link local scope
3   (unassigned)
4   (unassigned)
5   site local scope
6   (unassigned)
7   (unassigned)
8   organization local scope
9   (unassigned)
A   (unassigned)
B   (unassigned)
C   (unassigned)
D   (unassigned)
E   global scope
F   reserved
```

The same functionality was obtained in the MBONE by a careful tuning of the IPv4 TTL field. The IPv6 specification allows a much more precise definition. However, it obliges routers to enforce scope boundaries. In particular, the site and organization scopes can only be enforced if routers know which link belongs to what site and to what organization.

We should note that the scope indicator does not influence the meaning of a permanently assigned group. Consider, for example, the group identifier 43 (hex), which has been assigned to the *Network Time Protocol* (NTP) servers. We can decline it with five scopes, 1, 2, 5, 8, and E, to obtain five multicast addresses:

- FF01::43 represents all NTP servers on the same node as the sender.
- FF02::43 represents all NTP servers on the same link as the sender.
- FF05::43 represents all NTP servers in the same site as the sender.
- FF08::43 represents all NTP servers in the same organization as the sender.
- FF0F::43 represents all NTP servers in the Internet.

Unlike NTP, many groups can only be used within some limited scopes. For example, sending a message to "all dynamic hosts configuration servers on the Internet" would not make much sense.

3.2.2 Predefined Multicast Addresses

Group identifiers such as "all NTP servers" are normally allocated by the Internet Assigned Numbers Authority. They are generally hardwired in the application that characterizes the group. All network time management programs, for example, are expected to know that the address of "all NTP servers on the site" is FF05::43. They will declare their membership to this group when the program is started, exactly in the same way that members of a videoconference will join the multicast address that has been dynamically allocated to their group.

The IPv6 specification only defines four permanent group identifiers, which all IPv6 nodes are expected to understand:

- The group identifier 0 is reserved. It shall not be used with any scope.
- The group identifier 1 defines the *all IPv6 nodes* addresses. It can be used with a scope of 1, FF01::1, to identify all nodes on this node, or with a scope of 2, FF02::1, to identify all nodes on this link.
- The group identifier 2 defines the *all IPv6 routers* addresses. It can be used with a scope of 1, FF01::2, to identify all routers on this node, or with a scope of 2, FF02::2, to identify all routers on this link.
- The group identifier 10000 (hex) defines the group of *all dynamic host configuration servers* (DHCP servers and relays). It should be used with a scope of 2, FF02::1:0, to identify all DHCP servers and relays on this link.

The specification also reserves a range of multicast addresses, from FF02::1:0:0 to FF02::1:FFFF:FFFF, which is used by the IPv6 equivalent of the Address Resolution Protocol. We will present the usage of these addresses in Chapter 4.

3.2.3 Group Management

The IPv6's version of ICMP includes three group membership messages:

■ Type 130, Group Membership Query
■ Type 131, Group Membership Report
■ Type 132, Group Membership Termination

These are equivalent to the messages of IPv4's Internet Group Management Protocol, defined in RFC 1118. All these messages have the same format.

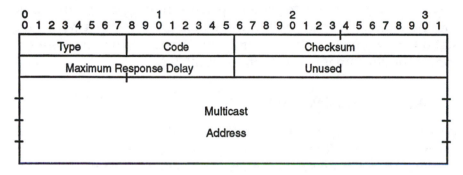

−   Format of Group Management ICMP Messages   −

The Type field will be set to 130, 131, or 132 for membership queries, reports, or terminations. The code will always be set to zero, as well as the unused field. The checksum is the regular ICMP checksum.

The procedure by which stations join a group is identical to that of IPv4. The router that wants to test the membership of a local station to groups sends a membership query; the stations that are members of a group respond by a *group membership report*.

The query may be focused on a specific group, in which case the packet will be sent to that group's address. The same address will be repeated in the ICMP's address field. Routers may also send broad queries directed to all groups. These queries will be sent to the link local all nodes multicast address, and the ICMP address field will be set to the unspecified address 0::0.

The reports sent by stations are always sent to the same group that is reported. That group's address is also copied in the ICMP message. The purpose of this procedure is to avoid duplicate reporting. Once a station reports its membership to the group, everybody else receives it and knows that there is no need to send an additional report. In the query messages, the maximum response delay field indicates the maximum time that responding report messages may be delayed, in milliseconds. Upon reception of the query, a station that wants to report its membership is supposed to draw at random a waiting delay, comprised between zero and this maximum response delay. It will then wait and either transmit if the delay elapses or shut up if another station sends a report before that delay. The maximum response delay is set to zero in report and termination messages.

The group membership terminations are sent by stations that leave a group in order to speed up the updating of the multicast routing tables. They are sent to the whole group so that remaining stations, if any, can immediately inform the routers that there are still some group members present on the local link.

3.2.4 Multicast Routing

We should carefully note that multicast routing in the Internet is still a topic of research. The query, report, and termination messages correspond to today's state of the art. They allow us to construct the equivalent of the IPv4 MBONE or to use an IPv6 version of the multicast extensions to OSPF. But we may expect to see a few changes in the coming years.

■ There is a project to add one or several source address fields in the Report to indicate that one wants to listen to a specific subset of sources within a group.

■ There is a similar project to add one or several source address fields in the termination to indicate that one is not interested in one or several of the group's members.

■ Certain multicast routing protocols require additional messages to determine which of the link's routers will relay the packets for a specific group. We may have to add an assert message to that effect, or we may have to add a preference field in the report message.

On the other hand, the extensions will clearly be upward compatible. IPv6 stations that follow the current spec will still be capable of joining and leaving groups.

3.2.5 Anycast

While multicasting has been happily tried by tens of thousands of IPv4 stations on the MBONE, anycasting was still a research project when the IPv6 specs were written. The principle of anycasting, in itself, is very simple. Instead of sending one packet to a specific server, one sends the packet to a generic address that will be recognized by all the servers of a given type, and one trusts the routing system to deliver the packet to the nearest of these servers. One could use anycasting to find out the nearest name server, the nearest file server, or the nearest time server.

There is no specific anycast format in IPv6. Anycast addresses are treated by hosts in exactly the same way as unicast addresses. The load is on the routing system, which has to maintain one route for each anycast address that is active in a given site. This is, however, conceptually very easy. In a distance vector protocol such as RIP, it is sufficient to add one entry per anycast address to the vector of destinations. In a link state protocol such as OSPF, one should create a special type of link state record that describes the presence of an anycast group member near one of the routers. We will describe in Chapter 4 how stations that host specific services can describe the service's anycast addresses to the local routers.

One expected usage of anycasting is *fuzzy routing*, for example, sending a packet at or through "one router of network X." This is still under study, because one has to define the associated management mechanisms. The IPv6 specification proposes, however, a limited step in that direction by defining the *subnet router* anycast address:

n bits	128-n bits
subnet prefix	0000000000000

The idea is that if a given prefix identifies a subnet, for example, an Ethernet, then all routers connected to that subnet should recognize the anycast address formed by appending to that prefix a null station identifier. This will allow stations to send packets to one of the subnet's routers. This particular type of anycasting does not require any extension to the routing tables, because there is already an entry for the subnet.

3.3 Interdomain Routing

Back in 1991, when the first efforts to define a new version of IP were started, we foresaw three possible "deaths of the Internet": the shortage of network numbers, the explosion of the routing tables and the overall shortage of IP addresses. Going to 128-bit addresses obviously solves the shortage of network numbers and IP addresses. There is room for trillions of networks and hosts. But just making the addresses larger does not by any means solve the explosion of the routing tables.

In today's Internet, if a router wants to compute the best routes toward all destinations, it has to maintain an entry for each network of the Internet in its routing table. Most routers do not, because the tables are already too large. They only maintain precise routing for a limited subset of the Internet, for example their business partners, and they use *default routes* to reach the other networks. But such simplifications cannot be used by the backbone routers in the transit networks of the Internet providers. They have to maintain complete tables. As a result, the providers have to continuously upgrade their configurations to cope with the growth of the Internet.

The solution to the explosion of the routing table is, however, well known. We must *aggregate* several routing entries. This supposes that we introduce some hierarchy for the addresses and that we deploy an interdomain routing technology that enables us to take advantage of this hierarchy. The planned solution for IPv6 is to use *provider addresses,* because these addresses have a good relation with the network's topology. Routes will be exchanged through the Interdomain Routing Protocol (IDRP). Users that have specific constraints will be able to build tunnels or to use the routing header to build up transit routes that fit their policy requirements.

3.3.1 From CIDR to Providers

The IPv6 addressing plans are largely based on the experience gained with IPv4 and CIDR. The managers of IPv4 networks are currently trying to curb the growth of the routing table by deploying classless interdomain routing (CIDR). Within CIDR, IPv4 addresses are no longer considered as composed of fixed-length network numbers, the old 8-bit class A, 16-bit class B, or 24-bit class C numbers. Network numbers are replaced by variable-length prefixes. The prefixes are supposedly assigned in a coordinated way, so that, for example, all the French prefixes start with the same high-order bits, a common prefix. If everything works according to plan, it will be possible to replace all the individual entries for French networks by the common prefix.

Networks, however, do not really follow country boundaries. It appears that the route used to reach a French network depends a lot on how this network is connected to the Internet. There are currently five large Internet providers in France, each of which uses its own set of international connections. Moreover, some large French users lease their own set of transatlantic lines and connect directly to U.S. providers. The same is true for every country, in fact every region and every city. Competition is the rule.

An addressing plan based on political or geographical boundaries would not allow aggregation. The route toward each network depends on its connection to the Internet. There is not one common route for a country, a region, or a city. There is thus no hope of having only one line in the routing table for all the networks within a country, region, or city.

The addressing plan will only allow aggregation if it reflects the network's topology. This is the main argument for choosing provider-based addresses for IPv6. By definition, all the customers of a single provider are routed through this provider's network. Outside this network, it is sufficient to enter a line per provider in the routing table. Basically, provider-based addressing solves the routing explosion problem by adding a provider layer on top of the network layer in the addressing hierarchy.

Not everybody agreed with the use of provider-based addressing. The main objection is that it creates a dependency between the customer and the provider. Suppose that I change my Internet access from provider A to provider B. My address prefix, assigned by A, was D000:A:0:123::/64. I have two solutions:

1. *Convince providers A and B to let me continue to use my old address,*

2. *Change all the addresses of all the stations within my network to reflect a new prefix assigned by B (e.g., D000:B:0:456::/64)*

In the first case, B will have to advertise to the whole Internet that the prefix D000:A:0:123::/64 should be routed through its own network, not through A. This means essentially that we will now have one line for my network in all the tables of all core routers around the world. If too many networks follow my example, the routing tables' explosion is guaranteed. In practice, these exceptions can only be tolerated for a very short period. I will have to renumber as soon as possible.

Suppose now that instead of changing from A to B, I decide to connect my network to these two providers. I have, again, several solutions:

1. *Consider that one of the providers, A, is my default server and convince B to let me use the address assigned by A*

2. *Partition my network so that some subnetworks are served by A and others by B*

3. *Assign two addresses to each station*

The third solution will allow each station to select providers on a connection per connection basis, maybe even on a packet per packet basis. This was almost impossible to implement with IPv4.

We will see in Chapter 4 how the automatic configuration procedures allow us to renumber IPv6 networks automatically and also to assign multiple addresses to each interface, typically one per provider. This will allow us to use provider-based addressing and to keep the routing table manageable, without binding customers to the hands of their providers.

3.3.2 From BGP-4 to IDRP

The building block of the IPv4 Internet is the *autonomous system,* a collection of subnetworks managed by a single entity. An autonomous system may be, for example, the network of an Internet Service Provider or that of one large company. It comprises many subnetworks, and it includes interior routing procedures for managing routing inside the autonomous system. Autonomous systems use Exterior Gateway Protocols (EGP) to exchange reachability information, to describe the destination for which they accept to relay packets. The first such protocol was actually named the Exterior Gateway Protocol (EGP). It was defined in 1982 and remained in use for almost 10 years before being gradually replaced by the successive versions of the Border Gateway Protocol (BGP).

The current version of BGP, BGP-4, supports the routing table aggregation procedures required by CIDR. It is a *path vector* protocol.

It allows border routers, which link two adjacent autonomous systems, to announce *paths*. A path is described by a set of attributes, notably the list of autonomous systems that it traverses and the list of network prefixes that it reaches. Listing all the transit systems is a sure way to detect loops, because a border router can easily refuse to consider a path that already passes through its own autonomous system. This allows the implementation of arbitrary routing policies, by which a system controls the list of destinations for which it will accept packets from a peer.

BGP was designed specifically for the Internet. It is optimized to handle 32-bit addresses, so much optimized in fact that BGP-4 could not be easily upgraded to handle IPv6. For this reason, the Exterior Gateway Protocol used by IPv6 is not based on BGP but rather on IDRP, the Inter-Domain Routing Protocol, which was first designed as a component of the Open System Interconnection family of protocols defined by the ISO. IDRP was considered a good candidate because:

■ Although defined within the OSI family, it does not show any dependency on OSI networking,

■ It was defined from the beginning for *multiprotocol routing* and is capable of computing tables for several families of addresses,

■ It is based on the same path vector family as BGP and includes, in fact, a superset of BGP's functionalities.

Actually, one could observe that most of the designers of IDRP were also involved in the design of BGP. They brought all their knowledge to this design. As a result, there is a very large consensus in the routing community for adopting IDRP instead of designing a BGP-5 or a BGP-6.

The most striking differences between BGP and IDRP lie in the vocabulary. IDRP is defined in the ISO standard 10747, and the real name is, according to ISO, the Protocol for Exchange of Inter-Domain Routeing Information among Intermediate Systems to Support Forwarding of ISO 8473 PDUs. The text uses strange names such as Border Intermediate Systems (a border gateway in BGP) or Network Protocol Data Units (a datagram). But, then, the new notation of Routing Domain is probably less arcane than the classic Internet equivalent, Autonomous System. Once we forego the initial impression of strangeness, we realize that there are only four important differences with BGP:

- While BGP messages are exchanged over a TCP connection, IDRP protocol units are carried over a bare datagram service.
- While BGP is a single-address-family protocol, IDRP may carry several types of addresses.
- While BGP uses 16-bit autonomous system numbers, IDRP identifies the domain by using variable-length address prefixes.
- While BGP describes the full list of autonomous system numbers that a path passes through, the IDRP concept of Routing Domain Confederations can be used to aggregate this information.

The decision to carry BGP messages over TCP had some advantages. It made the design of the protocol simpler by reducing the number of timers and procedures. It had, however, several inconveniences, because it introduced interactions between BGP routing decisions and TCP flow control and error control strategies. IDRP, on the other hand, includes its own control procedures. This is in accordance with modern protocol designs. If a message is lost, it makes more sense to build up a new message that describes the new state of routing than to repeat a string of bytes that described an already aging picture of the network. IDRP was initially designed to run over the simple datagram service provided by the network layer of the OSI suite, CLNP. But it is entirely straightforward to replace this datagram layer. For the Internet, IDRP will run directly on top of IPv6. IDRP packets will be identified by the payload number 45.

Within BGP-4, reachable destinations are identified by a length, expressed as a number of bits, and a prefix:

Length	(1 octet)
Prefix	(variable)

IDRP uses a slightly more complex format. Reachable destinations are identified by a three-component structure:

Address Family (2 octets)
Addr-length (2 octets)
Addr-info (variable)

The address family qualifies the address information. Examples of families can be ISO, using the 20-octet NSAP addresses; IPv4, using 32-bit addresses; or IPv6, using 128-bit addresses. Prefixes are indeed shorter than addresses. There is no necessity to transmit the trailing zeros. The address length expresses the number of octets that are actually transmitted. In the case of IPv6, prefixes are not constrained to fit on octet boundaries and the address information is actually comprised of two fields:

Length (1 octet)
Prefix (variable)

The first octet describes the number of bits in the prefix. It is followed by the number of octets necessary to encode these bits.

Address prefixes encode reachable destinations. In complement to address prefixes, BGP uses autonomous system numbers to identify the domains through which a packet sent on that path will be relayed. These numbers are encoded on 16 bits. Instead of numbers, IDRP uses IPv6 prefixes to identify routing domains. This has two advantages:

■ Sixteen-bit numbers can only encode 65,536 domains. This will not be enough when the Internet will include trillions of networks. On the contrary, there will always be as many IDRP prefixes as there are addresses.

■ Sixteen-bit numbers have to be assigned by the IANA, independently from addresses. Prefixes, on the contrary, are a by-product of the address assignment.

The usage of prefixes leads naturally to the fourth important advantage of IDRP over BGP. To prevent loops, BGP carries with each path a detailed list of all domains on the path. If two paths leading to neighboring destinations are aggregated, the list has to be the union of the two independent lists. A provider may aggregate all the paths leading to all its customer domains. All these destinations will be represented by a single entry in the routing table. But the autonomous system path attribute will have to include the complete list of all the customers' autonomous systems, severely reducing the benefits of aggregation. IDRP allows routing domains to be grouped together in confederations. A set of connected domains may choose to appear to the outside world as a single domain, a confederation, which will be identified by its own address prefix. In our example, the provider will represent all its customers' networks as well as its internal backbone by a single prefix for the outside world. Internally, on the contrary, it will provide detailed information for better loop control and path assessment. The confederation mechanism is inherently recursive: confederations can be confederated again to obtain larger and larger aggregates. With this mechanism, we may hope to achieve scalable routing in a very large Internet.

3.3.3 Provider Selection

Provider-based addresses have the advantage of being well fitted to the network's topology. But this is only a mixed blessing, especially if we consider the rigidities introduced by TCP. Suppose that a customer's network is connected to two different providers. Each station has two different addresses. When it starts a TCP connection, it picks one of these addresses, which will then be used for the duration of the connection. By doing so, it has tied the fate of the connection to that of the provider's network. The partner's responses will be sent to the chosen address, even if the provider's network is too expensive, congested or even broken.

The obvious solution here is to use the routing header to force packets to go through an alternative provider. The station has two addresses, say A:X and B:X through provider A and provider B. The packets are normally sent by its partner, Y, toward the address A:X. By inserting a routing header, Y can force the packets to follow a route toward B:X and then to A:X. Packets will still have the same source and final destination address, TCP will continue to work, but they will be routed through the provider B. The last hop, from B:X toward A:X will be entirely contained within the host X and will thus not add any transmission delay. The single drawback of this technique is the added overhead of a one-step routing header, that is, 64 bits of payload header and 128 bits of address.

In this example, the hosts make the decision to use one or the other provider. They do not always have sufficient information to do so. Network managers who want to concentrate the provider selection at the network boundary, in a border router, may choose to do so by establishing tunnels. This is especially useful when there is a desire to bypass the policy decisions taken by a direct provider. Tunnels may be either simple or routed. In the simple case, the IPv6 packet between X and Y is simply carried as the payload of another IPv6 packet between the border router B and the selected provider P:

IPv6 header. From B to P.	IPv6 header. From X to Y	End to end payload.

—   Simple Tunneling   —

More complex decisions can be obtained by using the routing header to establish tunnels through a specified set of providers (e.g., through P1, P2, P3):

IPv6 header. From B to P1	Routing header through P2, P3	IPv6 header. From X to Y	End to end payload.

—   Tunneling through a Source Route   —

Simple and complex tunneling may be facilitated by the use of anycast addresses. Without the use of anycast addressing, the border router B will have to pick the address of specific routers within P1, P2, and P3. The fate of the tunnel will be linked to the fate of these routers. But the providers may have selected and published unicast addresses that are recognized by all routers within their networks. These addresses will be chosen within the provider's address space. They will be indistinguishable from the address of a fictitious router right in the middle of the network and will not require any specific entry in the routing table. The advantage of using anycast addresses as intermediate points in source routes is obvious. There is no need to select exactly one router per network; the packets will always follow the shortest path even if the topology changes.

3.4 Intradomain Routing

An interior routing protocol is used to compute routes and maintain connectivity within a routing domain or autonomous system.

This is in line with the current Internet architecture in which domain managers have to choose an IGP. There is no need here to invent a new technology. It is preferable to build on experience and to simply adapt the routing protocols of IPv4. The IETF working groups are currently preparing updated versions of OSPF and RIP. We may also expect IPv6 extensions for other protocols (e.g., IS-IS and EIGRP).

3.4.1 Updating OSPF

OSPF (Open Shortest Path First) is the recommended protocol for intradomain routing. It is a link state protocol. All routers maintain a copy of a data base that contains link state records describing the status of the network, or rather the status of the network area to which they belong. This protocol has been in use for several years and has been constantly upgraded to better fit the needs of network managers. The IPv6 version of OSPF is a simple translation of the IPv4 version, making minimal changes to accommodate the new address format.

OSPF for IPv6 will be run on top of IPv6, between IPv6-capable nodes. The IPv6 link state data base will not be shared with the IPv4 data base. IPv4 OSPF and IPv6 OSPF will operate in parallel, following the "ships in the night" model, rather than trying to achieve integrated routing.

The IPv6 version is obtained by applying minimal changes to the IPv4 version, essentially replacing all occurrences of 32-bit IPv4 addresses with 128-bit IPv6 addresses:

■ The link state records will be identified by a 128-bit field, possibly an IPv6 address, in exactly the same way that the IPv4 link state records were identified by a 32-bit field.

■ The routers in the network will be identified by one of their 128-bit IPv6 addresses.

■ The network areas will be identified by a 128-bit field, possibly an IPv6 address or an IPv6 prefix.

■ The IPv6 OSPF will not use a 32-bit network mask to qualify the subnet prefixes. Instead, it will use a 32-bit integer to encode the number of bits in the length of the prefix.

These minimal changes guarantee that the IPv6 OSPF software can be easily derived from the IPv4 software. They also ensure that whoever knows how to configure OSPF for an IPv4 network will rapidly understand how to use the IPv6 version.

3.4.2 Updating RIP

There were some questions on the opportunity to create a version of RIP for IPv6. The simple distance vector technology of RIP is very inferior to the link state technology of OSPF. The length of a path is equal to the number of hops on the path, whatever the speed or delay of these hops. In some conditions, RIP relies on counting to infinity to eliminate loops: paths whose metrics exceed the conventional value of infinity are considered broken. The infinity is set to a relatively low value, 16, in order to avoid spending too much time during this counting. As a consequence, RIP cannot be used on a network where some paths are longer than 16 hops. In fact, the only advantage of RIP is that it is very simple and can thus be implemented in very cheap boxes that could not support a fully functional protocol such as OSPF. RIP can be used in networks that are small and simple, or in small areas at the fringes of an OSPF network.

The definition of RIP for IPv6 underwent several successive stages. At some point, some members of the group would have liked to update RIP so that it could use better metrics and include sophisticated loop detection. They could not get a consensus on that option. On the contrary, it was decided to perform the simplest possible updates to the original RIP protocol. The RIP packet format for IPv6 is a straightforward evolution of the IPv4 version.

In the version of RIP for IPv6, a packet is composed of a 32-bit header and a set of address + metric pairs describing reachable destinations. The initial header comprises a command code and a version field, which is set to 1 in the current version. As in RIP for IPv4, only two commands are defined, for requests and responses. Requests are sent to trigger an immediate response, to get a response about the status of a particular destination. Responses are also sent to all neighbors at regular 30-second intervals. Each destination is described by a 128-bit IPv6 address and a subnet mask, that is, an octet containing the number of valid bits in the address. The metric field, for each destination, indicates the number of hops necessary to reach this destination. It is possible to describe a default route by setting the address to the null value 0::0 and by setting the subnet mask to zero.

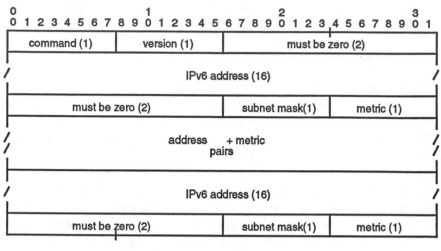

— Format of a RIP for an IPv6 Packet —

The RIP messages are exchanged by the RIP processes in UDP datagrams. The maximum length of a datagram is determined by the MTU of the link toward the neighbor. RIP processes are expected to place as many destinations in the message as fit the local MTU.

3.4.3 Other Protocols

OSPF and RIP are not the only routing protocols used in networks connected to the Internet. Some networks use the dual IS-IS protocol, and others use a proprietary protocol defined by cisco, IGRP.

The *dual IS-IS* is an extension of the routing protocol defined for CLNP in the OSI suite. It is a link state protocol as OSPF but, contrary to OSPF, it tries to perform integrated routing instead of relying on a simple "ships in the night" strategy. A single data base describes the links between all the network's routers. This network description is then completed by protocol-specific addressing information. If one wants to access a destination of address A in protocol family F, one first examines the addressing information to find out which router serves the address A. One then uses the generic information to compute the route toward that router. Dual IS-IS is currently capable of handling the OSI networking protocol, CLNP, in parallel with IPv4. Defining an extension for IPv6 is very simple and will probably be done by the IETF.

The initial version of *cisco's IGRP* is now somewhat outdated. It does not support variable-length subnets and is thus not compatible with CIDR addressing and routing. The extended version of IGRP, EIGRP, solves this problem and should be used instead. EIGRP, like IS-IS, is capable of supporting several network protocols in parallel. One may expect cisco to include IPv6 support in a future release of EIGRP.

3.5 Points of Controversy

The definition of the addressing and routing strategy for the new IP was indeed subject to many debates, some of which were very sour. There were in fact three points of contention. Many thought that the addresses should have a variable length, not a fixed one. Others complained strongly against the choice of provider-based addressing. Then there were quite a few routing specialists who thought that routing should be flow oriented and that the simple datagram strategy was not sufficient. Their objections were overruled, but are still quite interesting.

3.5.1 The Length of Addresses

The choice of 128-bit addresses for IPv6 is indeed a compromise. Among the main contenders in the IPng race, SIPP featured 64-bit addresses while TUBA used NSAP addresses whose length could vary between 1 and 20 octets. Several experts maintained that any fixed choice, however large, was in fact shortsighted. They would have liked to see a fully variable length. If there was a limit, that limit should have been very large, perhaps 255 octets. Their main arguments were the difficulty of predicting the size of the Internet and the need to support complex routing strategies.

Predicting how large the Internet will be by the year 2020 is indeed difficult. When the initial designers of the Internet chose the 32-bit address size, they were entirely convinced that 32 bits allowed billions of addresses, more than their wildest dream of growth. If we follow that line of reasoning, there is a chance that the Internet will be even larger that what we expect and that we will have to change again to an address size larger than 128 bits. But at that time the network will be so large that the transition will be even more painful than it is today. Why should we donate that problem to our grandchildren?

The argument was indeed taken into consideration during the final design choice of IPv6. The designers of SIPP were entirely convinced that 64 bits was enough. After all, 2 to the power 64 is an astronomically large number, more than ten billions of billions. Even if we take into account the address assignment efficiency of the current Internet (i.e., an *H* ratio of 0.21), we may reasonably expect to number more than two hundred thousands of billions of stations within 64 bits. But even if a choice of 64 bits would have been entirely rational, we had to compromise on 128 bits, which is sufficient to number billions of billions of billions of stations.

The second argument is more subtle. The idea is that, while the Internet will grow larger, it will also grow more complex. We will need to devote addressing bits to take this additional complexity into account, additional octets for each additional layer of hierarchy. The overall efficiency will be reduced and even 128 bits may end up not being enough.

Again, this argument was heard. It is the main reason behind the cautious address allocation strategy adopted for IPv6. Once we have a better understanding of the future network structure, we will be able to devise a better plan and to implement it in some of the reserved address space.

The opponents to variable-length addresses had two arguments, which, in the end, carried the decision. They believe that fixed-length addresses are simpler to manage and to implement. They also maintained that, even when the format is variable, usage results in practice in fixed-length addresses.

Fixed-length addresses result in fixed-length formats, which are certainly easier to program. Variable-length structures have to be explicitly managed. One needs to allocate variable amounts of memory, to free this memory. Each comparison, each format checking requires additional tests. The software becomes larger, slower, and more error prone. The classical counterargument is that these complex functions can be implemented by some specialized pieces of hardware. This may be true for dedicated boxes such as routers, but is much less obvious for personal computers or workstations that very seldom use this type of additional hardware. The consensus was that fixed formats were a good thing for most implementations.

We have, in fact, very little experience with variable-length addresses. The little experience we have had with the OSI suite and the NSAP addresses showed us that managers tend to use a fixed-length format even if the protocol allowed variable length. In practice, all NSAP are 20 octet. Moreover, because there is a general feeling that the addresses can be as long as needed, users tend to be careless and use more addressing bits than necessary. Again, the NSAP example shows that addresses end up including identifications of policies, allocation strategies, or format. These bits are only there to please politicians. They do not help routing. Instead of having short and fixed addresses, we end up having addresses that are almost fixed but longer. Changing the consensus size might very well be as traumatic as changing the address format itself.

After all these debates, it appears that 16 octets was a reasonable compromise. The longer size implies some amount of overhead, but it allows a very simple implementation of address configuration, making management easy and allowing "plug and play" functionalities.

3.5.2 Providers and Monopolies

The choice of a provider addressing was dictated by the need to curb the growth of the routing table. However, it is a departure from the current situation in which addresses belong to the users. Some large users have currently a large number of network providers. They have fears that the management of multiple provider addresses will be very cumbersome and very expensive.

The fears may well be grounded in the state of today's Internet. There is very little use of dynamic configuration protocols such as DHCP. Changing addresses is often very difficult. The price to pay for changing providers would thus be very high. It would outweigh the benefits of an increased service or a slightly reduced price. In practice, only very few customers would change providers. The market would be ossified. We will see in Chapter 4 that dynamic configuration will be a standard feature of IPv6. But it is hard to fight a current opinion, based on experience and the state of the art, with mere promises of a bright future.

Steve Deering did explore the geographic alternative to provider addressing as part of his design of SIP. In Steve's scheme, the world would be partitioned in a set of regions or *metropolitan areas*, which could be further organized by countries and continents. All providers serving a given area would be required to interconnect and to reroute packets to the provider serving each of the area's customer. Customers would retain their addresses when they change providers. The burden would be on the providers. They would manage larger routing tables, and they would have to interact tightly with other providers.

Steve's geographical addressing plan is not yet buried. In fact, a sizable part of the address space is reserved for geographic addresses. However, it will be hard to deploy any such system in the short term because most providers oppose it vehemently.

It might be more realistic to simply develop better configuration tools and also to update TCP so that it can change the addresses in use without breaking existing connections. This would probably be in line with the Internet philosophy of keeping the network simple and placing the complexity at the edges, in the end systems.

3.5.3 Flows and Services

The IPv6 routing architecture is by and large that of IPv4. Most of us see this as a good point and think that 20 years of success just proved it was right. Some specialists, on the other hand, believe that it does not provide the necessary controls for real-time applications. Instead of pure datagrams, we should be able to explicitly set up flows. In their opinion, routing should be intertwined with resource reservation.

The route taken by IP datagrams is determined by the destination address and the state of the routing tables. All datagrams follow the same route. In situations of congestion, this route may not provide a sufficient quality of service for a real-time application such as a videoconference. It could well happen, however, that another route to the destination would provide an acceptable service, even if this means some contorted routing. The users should have a way to force their packets to follow that alternative route.

The problem was not entirely ignored by the designers of IPv6. Applications could in fact use the routing header to source route the packets through the alternative path. But this poses two problems. First, the applications can only take efficient routing decisions if they have sufficient information about the network's state. Second, source routing results in very large headers and some inefficiency.

One way to obtain knowledge about the state of the network would be to maintain map servers, an Internet-wide version of the link state data bases maintained by OSPF or IS-IS. Applications would look at this map in much the same way that a car driver looks at the map of interstate routes. They would also get some information about congested areas, in much the same way that a car driver listens to the radio and learns about traffic jams. They would then pick a path that avoids congested areas and provides sufficient resources for supporting their application.

The path that the application chooses is expressed as a set of intermediate relays, a *source route*. But this source route may well include a large number of points, maybe a dozen or two. Multiply by 128 bits and you are left with very little space for the payload. To alleviate this overhead, the proponents of flows generally advocate a *flow setup model*, similar to those of X.25 virtual circuit networks. The explicit source route would only be carried during a setup phase. Further packets would only be tagged with the route identifiers.

The proposal to install such flows was politely listened to, but failed to convince the majority of the IETF. In fact, it goes contrary to one of the basic principles of Internet architecture, which is to avoid placing state in the routers. Besides, all this construction is a thought experiment. It has perhaps been well analyzed in its designers' brains, but it has never been tried and proved true. The first instantiation of this design in the Interdomain Policy Routing protocol (IDPR, not to be confused with IDRP) was so complex and so difficult to implement that it could never be deployed on a significant portion of the Internet. Nobody ever maintained an Internet-wide network map. Going to the flow-based network would be a jump into an unknown territory. Better stay with the existing architecture!

3.6 Further Reading

The complete description of the IPv6 addressing architecture will be found in a soon to be published RFC, "IP Version 6 Addressing Architecture" by Robert Hinden. The initial address allocation plan is described in the soon to be published RFC, "An IPv6 Global Unicast Address Format" by Yakov Rekhter, Peter Lothberg, Robert Hinden, Steve Deering, and Jon Postel.

I described the IPv4 routing algorithms such as RIP, OSPF, BGP and CIDR in my book *Routing in the Internet*, published by Prentice Hall in 1995. The book also covers extensions to the routing architecture for multicast, mobility, and real time. Further information can be obtained in the various RFCs describing these protocols, notably

RFCs 1387, 1388 (RIP); RFCs 1583, 1587 (OSPF); RFC 1654 (BGP-4); and RFC 1338 (CIDR). The design of IDPR is explicated in a communication by Yakov Rekhter, Deborah Estrin, and Steve Hotz to the 1992 SIGCOMM conference, "Scalable Inter-Domain Routing Architecture," which was published in October 1992 in the *ACM Computer Communication Review*. IDPR itself is described in the ISO standard 10747, "Protocol for Exchange of Inter-Domain Routing Information among Intermediate Systems to Support Forwarding of ISO 8473 PDUs." The adaptation of IDRP, OSPF, and RIP to IPv6 is described in three memos that should soon be published as RFCs, "IDRP for IPv6" by Yakov Rekhter and Paul Traina, "OSPF IPv6 Extensions" by Fred Baker and Rob Coltun, and "RIPng for IPv6" by Gary Malkin.

The IPv6 multicast is largely based on the IPv4 version. The basic group management protocol is described in RFC 1112. The multicast extensions to OSPF are described in RFCs 1584 and 1585. The best reading for the basic theory of multicast routing in the Internet is still Steve Deering's Ph.D. thesis *Multicast Routing in a Datagram Internet Work*, Stanford University, 1991. Numerous research papers have been published describing practical proposals for scalable multicast routing in the Internet, notably a communication by Tony Ballardie, Paul Francis, and Jon Crowcroft to the SIGCOMM 1993 conference, *Core Based Trees* and a communication by Deborah Estrin and several coauthors to the SIGCOMM 1994 conference, *An Architecture for Wide-Area Multicast Routing*.

The debates on the various addressing possibilities took place on the "big-internet" electronic distribution list (big-internet@munnari.oz.au). The archives of this list are available on the Internet.

4

Plug and Play

B y the end of June 1994, the IPng saga was coming to a close. The IPng selection committee had almost made up its mind. The choice had to be based on the SIPP proposal, but SIPP could not be bought lock, stock, and barrel. A substantial number of directorate members thought that the 64-bit addresses were too narrow, that they would not provide enough flexibility to implement proper routing protocols. There was a compromise in sight, if only the SIPP proponents would agree to increase the address size to 128 bits. The IETF decision process is based on building consensus, part of which implies polling opinion leaders. I was one of those leaders by this time, or so they thought, so they polled me. Would I accept inflating the address to 128 bits? I had publicly stated many times that 64 bits was more than enough and I could back my opinion with substantial mathematical analysis. However, I did not hesitate too long. Going to 128 bits was a little price to pay to reach consensus and save the Internet. Moreover, 128-bit addresses have a definite advantage. They have twice the width that routing procedures require, hence they make a lot of room available for proper implementation of autoconfiguration procedures.

4.1 Autoconfiguration

Autoconfiguration is a long and somewhat abstract word. Literally, *autoconfiguration* means that a machine, a computer, will automatically discover and register the parameters that it needs to use in order to connect to the Internet. We used to refer to this problem through two metaphors, the "dentist office" and the "thousand computers on the dock."

Networking specialists imagine that dentists are rich enough to buy several computers, but that they have been trained in dentistry, not computer networks, so they can do little else than take the machine out of the box, plug in the various connectors, switch it on, and expect it to work. A requirement of IPv6 is that this should indeed be sufficient, even if the dentist is not connected to the Internet and even if there is no router in the office's network.

Network managers often have a dream, a bad dream. A thousands computers have just been delivered and are waiting on the unloading dock. It is 2 P.M. on Friday and the company expects that the entire network will be available by the end of the afternoon. This certainly implies that we will not have much time to configure each of these computers. It should be as automatic as possible.

As the specification progressed, other needs appeared, notably after the adoption of provider addressing. Just setting up the machine once and forever is not sufficient. One should also be able to change addresses dynamically as one changes provider and to obtain several addresses simultaneously when the network is connected to several providers. Then security and management requirements come into consideration. Some sites want more control than others; they want to be able to turn off the autoconfiguration capabilities. Finally, several important design decisions were taken. Address configuration would be an integral part of any IPv6 implementation. It would come both in a stateless mode and in a stateful mode, the latter using an IPv6 version of DHCP. Addresses would be assigned to interfaces for a limited lifetime.

4.1.1 Link Local Addresses

As soon as an interface is initialized, the host can build up a link local address for this interface by concatenating the well-known link local prefix and a unique token, a number that is unique to this host on this link. The model of the unique token is indeed the 48-bit Ethernet address.

Ethernet addresses are supposedly unique worldwide. This is a design decision made by the inventors of Ethernet in the late 1970s, at Xerox Parc. Knowing that the interface comes out with a unique address means that one can plug it into any Ethernet cable anywhere and be assured that there will not be any collision. The advantages are simpler network management and the possibility to connect Ethernet segments by *learning bridges*. Worldwide uniqueness is guaranteed by Xerox. The company will sell ranges of addresses to the manufacturers of Ethernet interfaces. The manufacturers then program each interface with its own, worldwide unique address.

The Ethernet solution was adopted by the 802 committee of IEEE. They generalized its usage to many different local networks such as token rings, FDDI rings, or radio networks. The 48-bit Ethernet addresses are generally referred to as IEEE-802 addresses. A typical link local address will be of the form

FE80:0:0:0:0:XXXX:XXXX:XXXX

In this notation, XXXX:XXXX:XXXX should indeed be replaced by the IEEE-802 address of the interface.

There may be some networks for which no IEEE-802 address is available. The implementors will have to derive the unique token from other elements, for example, the serial number of the computer board or the address assigned to the interface by the local network manager. The last resort may be to simply pick a number at random. After all, if there are a thousand hosts in the local network and if each picks a 48-bit number at random, the chances of at least one collision are about one in 300 million.

Link local addresses can only be used on the local link. They may well solve the dentist's problem, but they will not be sufficient for organizing a large network.

4.1.2 Stateless Autoconfiguration

IPv6 nodes start initializing their behavior by joining the *all nodes* multicast group. This is done by programming their interfaces to receive all the packets sent to the corresponding multicast address, FF02::1. They will then send a solicitation message to the routers on the link, using the *all routers* address, FF02::2, as destination and their own link local address as source. The hop count will be set to 255. We will explain why this is in section 4.2.7.

Type	Code	Checksum
Reserved		
Options ---		

–   Format of an ICMP Solicitation Message   –

A *solicitation message* is an ICMP message of type 133. The ICMP code is set to zero and the checksum is computed according to the usual procedure for ICMP messages. The solicitation message may include options, which are encoded in a type-length-value format, using one octet for the type, one octet for the length, and a variable number of octets for the value itself. The only option that is expected in the solicitation message is the link layer address of the source, for example its Ethernet or token ring address.

Type	Length	Link Layer Address ---

–   Format of the Source Address Option   –

The source *link layer address* option is identified by the type 1. The length is expressed in units of 64 bits or eight octets. For IEEE-802 addresses, the length will be set to 1 and the option's value will be composed of six octets, the 48-bit address. When the routers receive such a solicitation, they are supposed to reply with a router advertisement message. This message will be sent toward the link layer address of the requestor, using the content of the source address option as media address.

Type		Code		Checksum
Max Hop Limit	M	O	Reserved	Router Lifetime
Reachable Time				
Reachable Retrans Timer				
Options ---				

–   Format of an ICMP Router Advertisement Message   –

Router advertisements are ICMP messages of type 134. The ICMP code is set to zero, and the checksum is computed according to ICMP rules. The messages contain several parameters that can be found either at a fixed position in the advertisement header or as variable-length options. These parameters are used both for managing auto-configuration and for *neighbor discovery*, the IPv6 procedure that replaces both the IPv4 protocols of address resolution and router discovery. We will reexamine these messages in the presentation of neighbor discovery, in the next section of this chapter.

The parameters used by the address configuration procedures are two control bits, noted M and O, and the *prefixes* option. The *managed address configuration* bit is set to 0 when the stations are authorized to perform stateless autoconfiguration. If it is set to 1, the stations should not attempt to build up addresses themselves, but should contact an address configuration server, using a stateful protocol. The *other configuration* flag is set to 1 when the stations can do stateless address configuration, but should contact a config-uration server for obtaining other parameters. When the M bit is null, the station will examine the list of prefixes encoded as options.

Type	Length	Prefix Length	L	A	Reserved1
Valid Lifetime					
Preferred Lifetime					
Reserved2					
Prefix					

The Prefix Information Option

The *prefix information option* is identified by the option type 3. There may be several prefix options in a message, each of which encodes one separate prefix using 32 octets, or four 64-bit words. The length field is always set to 4. The prefix is encoded by a 128-bit address and by a prefix length expressed as a number of bits. The valid and preferred lifetime indicates the number of second before the address may be invalidated or deprecated. Two 1-bit flags qualify the prefix. The *on-link* bit, L, is set when the prefix is specific to the local link, when it can be entered in the list of local prefixes used by the neighbor discovery procedures. The *autonomous configuration* bit, A, is set when the prefix may be used for autonomous address configuration. In this case, the station will construct an address by replacing the last bits of the prefix by the interface's unique token, typically by the 48-bit IEEE-802 address. This can indeed only be done if the prefix is not too long. If the prefix includes more than 80 significative bits, it would be erroneous to replace the last 48 bits by an IEEE-802 address! In this case, the prefix will be ignored.

The router advertisement messages are not only sent in response to solicitations. Routers will also transmit them at regular intervals on the *all hosts* multicast address. If they receive a solicitation at a moment when the interval between repetitions has almost expired, they may choose to respond by multicasting their advertisement instead of sending it to just one station.

The station that has sent a solicitation is supposed to wait for a response. To protect itself against transmission errors, it will repeat its solicitation if it does not receive a response after a reasonable delay, for example after 2 seconds. However, it should not repeat the solicitation more than three times. Failure to receive a response after three solicitations indicates that there is probably no router on the link. The station can only communicate with other stations connected on the same link, as in the dentist office case. It should only use its link-local address.

4.1.3 Duplicate Detection

The autoconfiguration procedure can only work if a unique token is assigned to each interface. In principle, most interfaces come out with an IEEE-802 address. These addresses are worldwide unique and should thus form perfectly adequate tokens. But errors may occur, because some manufacturers of very low cost devices are known to use unregistered IEEE-802 numbers, leading to potential collisions. Then there is always the case of odd networks that do not use IEEE-802 addressing. Resorting to random numbers may cause problems, in particular when the random generators are not well behaved. Because duplicate address can cause severe problems, it is important to detect and report these errors as soon as possible.

The detection of duplicate addresses uses the neighbor discovery procedures. Once an address has been configured, the host sends a solicitation message toward that address and waits for one second. If another station has been configured with the same address, it will reply and advertise its link layer address, exposing the collision. At this point, the host will know that its number is not unique and that the corresponding addresses should not be used. It will then either pick a new number, if that is possible, or display an error message and ask for human intervention.

This procedure is not perfect. The absence of a reply may be caused by the absence of a collision, but it may also be due to the loss of the initial solicitation or of the reply itself. Stations are supposed to retry the procedure several times before being reasonably sure of the uniqueness of their token. These trials should be sufficiently spaced not to cause link layer congestions. According to the current specification, the message should be sent only once, after a delay chosen at random between 0 and 3 seconds.

4.1.4 Stateful Configuration

Stateless configuration has many advantages. It is very simple to use and does not require any servers. It has, however, two inconveniences, a relatively inefficient use of the address space and a lack of network access control.

Stateless autoconfiguration is based on unique tokens that tend to be 48 bits long. Using 48 bits for a single Ethernet segment is not very efficient, especially if we consider that the whole Internet today uses 32-bit addresses. We may consider that this addressing inefficiency is a small price to pay for simpler management, that each customer network will have at least 64 bits of address space, and that the remaining 16 bits are more than enough to number all the customer subnetworks. But the managers of very large networks may have a different opinion. They may want to use an internal addressing hierarchy that will require much more than 16 bits. If addresses are assigned by servers, they could be made arbitrarily short, for example, using only 8 bits per segment if less than 256 computers are connected to the segment.

Stateless autoconfiguration may also ease the task of spies and hackers. The whole idea of plug and play is that the legitimate user takes the machine out of the box, plugs it in, and runs. This also means that if hackers manage to carry computers within the premises, they will be able to just plug them in and run as if they were legitimate local users. One may well argue that this is already the case, that it suffices for the hacker to use the address of one of the local machines that happens to be silent at the time of the intrusion. One may further argue that real security has to involve authentication and encryption, that just disabling autoconfiguration is not very useful. But some managers will insist on enforcing administrative controls nevertheless.

The routers' advertisements may specify that the host should use *stateful configuration* by setting up the *managed configuration* bit. If the host receives a message as to where this bit is set, it should solicit the nearest address server. Isolated hosts will not receive any router advertisement. They should also try to contact a local address server.

The stateful configuration protocol is an IPv6 version of the IPv4 Dynamic Host Configuration Protocol (DHCP). This protocol will be upgraded to deliver IPv6 addresses as well as IPv4 addresses. The multicast address FF02::1:0 has been reserved for the group of all DHCP servers. It should be used to discover the local server.

4.1.5 Lifetime of Addresses

For a very long time, Internet users believed that they owned their IPv4 address, their network number. We saw in Chapter 3 that this cannot be the case anymore. One should be able to aggregate network numbers, which implies a dependency between addresses and network topology.

Network topology can change in many ways. Customers may change providers, company backbones may be reorganized, or providers may merge or split. If the topology changes with time and if the addresses must somehow reflect the topology, then addresses will have to change from time to time.

Addresses obtained through either stateless or stateful configuration will have a limited lifetime. In the stateful configuration, the lifetime will be indicated by the address server. In the stateless configuration, the lifetime of the address will be deduced from the lifetime of the prefix, as indicated in the routers' advertisement.

An address whose lifetime has expired becomes invalid. It shall not be used anymore as a source address by the local host nor as a destination address by its partners. This can have very harsh consequences on ongoing communications. TCP connections, for example, are established between a pair of Internet addresses. If one address becomes invalid, the TCP connection will be interrupted. The only ways to alleviate this are to change the TCP and to avoid using addresses that will soon become invalid.

The address configuration working group of the IETF had no mandate to change TCP, but it did insert a mechanism that makes it easier to predict that one address will shortly become invalid. IPv6 addresses will have two lifetimes, the valid lifetime and the preferred lifetime. An address whose valid lifetime has expired should not be used at all. An address whose preferred lifetime has expired becomes invalid. It should not be used for starting new connections. When a TCP process starts a connection, it knows the destination address, but can choose any of the local addresses as source address. It should pick the one that has the longest preferred lifetime or, at a minimum, it should avoid using any address that is already deprecated or that will very soon be deprecated.

Hosts are expected to continuously receive router advertisements. They will examine the prefixes contained in these advertisements. If the prefix is already known, they will use the valid and preferred lifetimes contained in the advertisement to update the one they that stored when the corresponding address was autoconfigured. If they learn a new prefix, if the autonomous configuration flag is set, they will autoconfigure a new address. This way the set of addresses attached to each interface is expected to continuously evolve.

Both valid and preferred lifetimes may be set to infinity, a conventional value encoded as 32 one bits. In this case, the address will never be invalidated or deprecated. This is by definition the case of the link local address, which will remain permanently valid.

4.1.6 Updating the Name Servers

Host configuration requires more than just address configuration. We will see that the neighbor discovery procedures allow hosts to configure key parameters such as the local subnetwork prefixes or the addresses of the local routers. But normal Internet operation also requires that the host learn its name. This name and the host's addresses should be registered in the Domain Name Service (DNS).

A normal complement to dynamic address configuration is dynamic update of the DNS. This procedure is currently being studied in the IETF.

4.2 Address Resolution

To transmit Internet packets on a particular subnetwork on a particular media, the Internet stations must determine the subnet address or media address of the target station. When Steve Deering wrote the initial specification of SIP, he assumed that SIP would rely on the same Address Resolution Protocol (ARP) as IPv4. But further work in the SIP, SIPP, and IPv6 working groups led to the development of the neighbor discovery procedure that encompasses the functions of ARP as well as those of router discovery.

A characteristic of IPv6 neighbor discovery is that it is defined in generic terms as part of IPv6 ICMP. This is a major difference from IPv4, for which a different address resolution protocol could be defined for each new media. There is indeed a matter of chicken and egg here. ICMP messages, like any IPv6 messages, can only be transmitted if the host knows the media address of their destination. This is solved by the use of multicast transmission. As long as the media address of the destination remains unknown, the messages are sent to multicast addresses. The media-level multicast address is supposed to be determined by an algorithm that may vary from media to media. For media of the IEEE-802 family such as Ethernet or FDDI, the 48-bit multicast address is obtained by concatenating a fixed 16-bit prefix, 3333 (hexadecimal), and the last 32 bits of the IPv6 multicast address. This prefix has been reserved by Xerox for use with IPv6.

33	33	DST13	DST14	DST15	DST16

Mapping of a Multicast Address in IEEE-802 Networks

The descriorption of the neighbor discovery procedures will assume that the host maintains four separate caches:

- The destinations' cache has an entry for each destination address toward which the host recently sent packets. It associates the IPv6 address of the destination with that of the neighbor toward which the packets were sent.

- The neighbors' cache has an entry for the immediately adjacent neighbor to which packets were recently relayed. It associates the IPv6 address of that neighbor with the corresponding media address.

- The prefix list includes the prefixes that have been recently learned from router advertisements.
- The router list includes the IPv6 addresses of all routers from which advertisements have recently been received.

In the remainder of this section, we will assume that these tables are present when we describe the basic discovery procedures.

4.2.1 The Basic Algorithm

To transmit a packet, the host must first find out the next hop for the destination. The next hop shall be a neighbor directly connected to the same link as the host. The host should then find a valid media address for that neighbor.

In many cases, a packet will already have been sent to the destination, and the neighbor address will be found in the destinations' cache. If this is not the case, the host will check whether one of the cached prefixes matches the destination address. If this is the case, the destination is local; the next hop is the destination itself. In the other cases, the destination is probably remote. The host should then select a router from the table of routers and use it as the next hop.

Once the next hop has been determined, the corresponding entry is added to the destinations' cache, and the neighbors' cache is looked up to find the media address of that neighbor. At this stage, there are four possibilities:

1. *If there is no entry for that neighbor in the cache, the host should send a neighbor solicitation message. The neighbor is then added to a new cache line whose status is set to* incomplete.

2. *If there is already an entry for that neighbor, but its status is incomplete, the host should wait for the completion of the procedure to learn the media address and send the packet.*

3. *If there is a complete line in the cache for the neighbor, the media address is known and the packet can immediately be sent.*

4. *If the neighbor's entry in the cache has not been refreshed for a long time, its status is suspect. The media address can be used, but a neighbor solicitation message should be sent.*

The *neighbor solicitation* messages are ICMP messages of type 135. The code is set to zero, and the checksum is computed according to ICMP rules. The target address parameter is set to the address of the solicited neighbor. The option field should contain the media address of the soliciting host encoded as a source link-level address option, as in the router solicitation message.

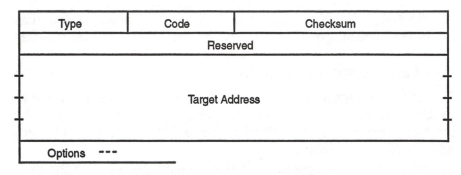

Type	Code	Checksum
Reserved		
Target Address		
Options ---		

—   Format of the Neighbor Solicitation Message   —

The IPv6 source address of the solicitation messages is always set to the link local address of the interface, and the hop count is always set to 1. The destination address, however, is not the IPv6 address of the solicited neighbor but a multicast address derived from it, the *solicited node multicast address*. The media address used for sending this ICMP message will be derived from this multicast address.

The solicited node multicast address is formed by concatenating a fixed 96-bit prefix, FF02:0:0:0:0:1, and the last 32 bits of the node's IPv6 address. All nodes are expected to compute the solicited node multicast addresses corresponding to each of their configured addresses, including the link local address, and to join the corresponding multicast groups.

The solicitation message will be received by all hosts that have at least one address whose last 32 bits match those of the solicited neighbor's address. Each of them will examine the target address parameter. If it matches one of its addresses, the solicited host will reply with a *neighbor advertisement* message. The advertisement is sent back to the solicitor's IPv6 address, using the link layer address specified in the solicitation. The source address should normally be the solicited IPv6 address, but there can be some exceptions, which we will detail in the next section.

The *neighbor advertisement* messages are ICMP messages of type 136. Their target address parameter is the solicited target address.

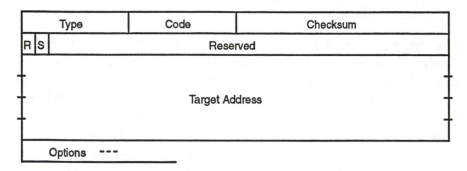

Type	Code	Checksum

| R | S | Reserved |

Target Address

Options ---

Format of the Neighbor Advertisement Messages —

They contain the media address of the target in a *target link layer address* option, whose format is identical to that of the source link layer address option except for the type field. Target address options have the type 2. The second 32-bit word of the ICMP message starts with two 1-bit flags. The router flag is set to 1 when the solicited node is a router. The solicited flag is set to 1 when the advertisement is sent in response to a solicitation.

When the soliciting host receives the advertisement message, it updates the corresponding entry in its neighbor cache. The entry is now complete, the neighbor is reachable, and packets can be transmitted.

IPv6 stations may in some circumstances send unsolicited advertisements. In this case, the destination will be set to the all nodes multicast address and the S bit will be set to 0. Solicitations and advertisements may also be exchanged during the address configuration procedures in order to detect duplicate addresses. When a host wants to check whether a target address is already in use on the link, it sends a solicitation message for that address. In order not to cause potential confusions, this solicitation differs from the normal message by two specificities:

■ The IPv6 source address is set to the unspecified address 0::0.

■ The source link-level address option is absent.

If a solicitation is received from an unspecified address, the response will be sent to the all nodes multicast address and the solicited flag will be set to 0.

4.2.2 Redirects

The procedure used by hosts to find the next hop is very simple. There will be cases when the hosts will pick the wrong next hop, for example, if there are several routers connected to the link but they send the packet to the wrong one, or if they send the packet to a router although the destination is in fact connected to the same link. Picking the wrong next hop is an error, albeit a benign one. The router that receives the misdirected packet will retransmit it to the correct next hop. The packet will eventually reach its destination, but it will be transmitted twice on the local link.

After redirecting the packet to the correct destination, the router may send a redirect message to the host so that the next message sent to that destination travels only once on the local network.

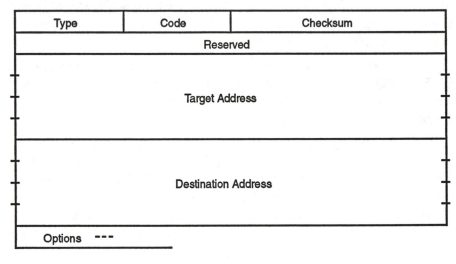

Type | Code | Checksum
Reserved
Target Address
Destination Address
Options ---

— Format of a Redirect Message —

The *redirect messages* are ICMP messages of type 137). They contain two address parameters. The destination address is that of the offending packet that triggered the redirection. The target address is that of a better next hop for that destination. The message may contain the media address of this next hop, encoded as a *target link layer address* option. It may also contain a copy of the first bytes of the offending packet, encoded as a redirected header option.

Type	Length	Reserved
Reserved		
IP header + data		

Format of the Redirected Header Option

The *redirected header option* is identified by the type 4. The length parameters expressed the number of 64-bit words that were copied from the redirected packet. It may be used by the host to correlate the redirection message with a previously sent packet, in the same way that other ICMP messages may be correlated with previous packets.

When a host receives a redirect message, it should update the destination's entry in its destination cache, replacing the erroneous next hop by the suggested value. If the target link layer address option is present, the host will also update the next hop's entry in the neighbors' cache.

4.2.3 The Case of Nonconnected Networks

The neighbor discovery algorithm relies on the presence of routers, especially as a fallback next hop when the destination is not recognized as local. The host's should, however, also be capable of operating in routerless environments, such as dentists' offices.

The absence of a router will be easily recognized by the hosts, because they will never receive any router advertisement. The router list and the prefix list will remain empty. In this situation, the hosts should only use their link local addresses as source addresses. It may well occur, however, that some stations on the same link have been configured with other addresses, either manually or by using a configuration server. A typical example would be that of anycast addresses.

In the absence of routers, the hosts will simply consider all addresses to be local. The next hop for any destination will be that destination itself. If it happens to be connected to the same link, the link layer address will be discovered and packets will be exchanged.

4.2.4 Getting Information from Routers

In connected networks, the hosts listen to router advertisements which provide them with several informations. We already examined the router advertisement messages in the previous section, but we only considered the parameters that address configuration procedures use. The header includes several other parameters, either for controlling transmission or for controlling cache behavior. These parameters are completed by three possible options, the source link layer address of the router, the link's MTU, and the prefixes.

Type	Code		Checksum
Max Hop Limit	M O	Reserved	Router Lifetime
Reachable Time			
Reachable Retransmission Timer			
Options - - -			

— Format of an ICMP Router Advertisement Message —

The *source link layer* option allows routers to advertise their media address so that each host will not need to send a neighbor solicitation message to the router.

The *max hop limit* is an 8-bit unsigned integer. It is programmed by a network manager as a parameter of the router's interface and is passed by routers to hosts as a suggestion of a reasonable value to use when sending IPv6 packets.

The *MTU option* is transmitted by routers that operate on links, such as token rings, that do not have a well-defined MTU. The router advertisement provides an easy vehicle for managers who want to specify a value common to all hosts. This option is encoded on exactly 64 bits (length = 1) and is identified by the option type 5.

Type	Length	Reserved
MTU		

— Format of the MTU Option —

The *router lifetime* parameter is a 16-bit integer. It indicates the number of seconds during which the advertising router could be held in the hosts' router lists, to be used as a default router.

The *reachable time* is a 32-bit integer. It indicates the time, in milliseconds, during which any neighbor is expected to remain reachable after it has somehow advertised its media address. It may be set to zero if the router does not want to indicate a specific value.

The *reachable retransmission timer* is a 32-bit integer. It indicates the interval, in milliseconds, between successive solicitations of a neighbor that is not returning solicited neighbor advertisements. Here again, a value of zero means that the router does not want to specify a value. Each advertisement has a lifetime (default 10 minutes).

4.2.5 Black Hole Detection

IPv6 includes automatic autoconfiguration and router discovery procedures. The reference implementation that we described uses caches to remember the results of next hop computation and redirects as well as the media addresses of neighbors. There is always a risk that these procedures will go afoul and that the station ends up sending packets to a router that is not operational anymore, to a media address that is not connected anymore. The result would be a black hole. Packets will be sent toward a dead end they will be lost somewhere in an electronic limbo. It is thus very important to check that the information present in the various caches is still valid. This is the role of the *neighbor unreachability detection* procedures defined as part of IPv6 neighbor discovery.

A host can often learn that a destination is reachable without any specific procedure. The most obvious case is when the packets sent on a TCP connection between that host and the destination are regularly acknowledged or, in fact, when any upper-level connection is making progress. In that case, the TCP process or the upper-level process can pass *reachability indications* to the IPv6 process, indicating that the corresponding entries in the destinations' and neighbors' caches are still valid. Some applications are, however, strictly unidirectional. If a host is sending video packets over UDP, it probably does not expect acknowledgments. In that case, the entry in the neighbor cache will age.

When no confirmation has been received for a reachable time interval, by default 30 seconds, the entry in the neighbor cache becomes dubious. The entry can still be used for sending a few packets. A few seconds after transmitting the next packet, the host should actively seek confirmation of the neighbor's reachability by sending a solicitation message. If the neighbor responds with a solicited advertisement, the reachability is confirmed and the entry may remain in the cache for another reachable time interval. Note that only solicited advertisements, explicitly addressed to the solicitor, count. Receiving a multicast message only proves one-way connectivity. It does not prove that the solicited host receives the solicitor's messages.

If the solicitation fails, it can be repeated a few times. If no response arrives in that interval, the neighbor is considered unreachable. Packets bound to that neighbor will be discarded, and an ICMP message will be sent back to indicate unreachability. The corresponding entry is removed from the neighbor's table and a new next hop must be computed for all the destinations that were reached through that neighbor.

If some of the routers in the routers' list are unreachable, the host should indeed not choose them as the next hop for default destination. If all routers are unreachable, the host should try each in turn so that they will all be tested for reachability.

A particular case of unreachability may occur when a station ceases to behave as a router and becomes a simple host, when its routing capabilities are disabled. This station will still respond to solicitations, but the hosts should examine the router flag (R) in the advertisements. If the host believes that the station was the router but receives an advertisement in which the R flag is null, it should remove the corresponding entry from the list of routers. It should also choose a new next hop for all the entries that were previously reached through that router.

4.2.6 Random Delays

The neighbor discovery procedures use a number of timers and repetitions. In many cases, some messages have to be repeated at regular intervals. This is the case for router advertisements and solicitation messages during the duplicate detection procedure or the unreachability detection procedure. To avoid simultaneous transmission of messages by multiple sources and the resulting peaks of traffic and collisions on the wire, the value of these intervals is not fixed, but chosen at random between a minimum and a maximum. Examples of random intervals are

■ The interval between successive transmission of router advertisements in order to avoid synchronization between all routers.

■ Advertisements sent by routers in response to solicitations may be delayed by a small random value in order to avoid simultaneous arrival of multiple advertisements at the soliciting host. If the advertisements are multicast, they must be delayed.

■ Hosts should wait for a small random delay before sending their initial solicitations. If many hosts are initialized at the same time, for example, after a power failure, the small delay will avoid a solicitation storm.

The random values, or rather the pseudorandom values, are generally provided by a pseudorandom number generation algorithm. This pseudorandom number generator should indeed be designed to be as random as possible. Obviously, if all stations used the same algorithm and initialized it at the same time with the same values they would all obtain the same sequence of pseudorandom numbers. This would result in undue synchronizations and collisions. A reasonable precaution is to seed it with node-specific numbers, for example, the Ethernet address of the interface or the serial number of the computer.

4.2.7 Protection Against Off-link Messages

The reliance on ICMP messages for neighbor discovery introduces a potential risk. Vile hackers, from a part of the Internet of which you had not heard before, could send forged router advertisements or redirect messages to your machine, playing havoc with local routing and address assignment.

The "off-link" menace is eliminated by a clever choice of the hop-count, suggested by Bob Gilligan. The hop-count of all address confirguration and neighbor discovery messages will be set to the maximum value, 255.

This is harmless, because these messages will never be relayed. It is also a very powerful test. As the hop count is decremented by every relay, only local packets may arrive with a hop-count of 255. By discarding incoming neighbor discovery packets whose hop-count is not set to 255, hosts will effectively progress themselves against off-links attacks.

4.3 Advanced Features

A typical routing domain contains several types of local networks interconnected through other networks and serial links. The basic neighbor discovery procedure is designed for simple hosts connected to multicast capable links such as Ethernet or Token Ring. It can, however, be adapted very easily to point to networks, and a restricted version can be run over switched networks that are not multicast capable.

Neighbor discovery procedures can also handle special configurations such as proxyservers, anycast servers, or multihomed hosts.

4.3.1 Serial Links

A serial link can be considered to be a network connecting exactly two stations. A local link address can be trivially assigned. It suffices to allocate a unique number to each interface. If both stations are hosts, they can communicate by using the local link addresses. If one station is a router, it can send router advertisements to the host, thus enabling automatic address configuration. If both stations are routers, they are expected to synchronize their routing functions by running a routing protocol such as RIP or OSPF, or IDRP if they belong to different domains.

4.3.2 Nonbroadcast Multiple Access

Most internauts will tell you that circuit switching is not very well adapted to data transmission. Packet switched networks such as Ethernet or FDDI are a better fit for the Internet Protocol than circuit switched networks such as telephone networks, ISDN, X.25, or ATM. We can indeed run IPv6 over switched circuits, but this will always require some degree of manual configuration.

Switched networks are generally provided by telecommunication companies. Internet users buy switched circuits in order to provide semipermanent connections between two distant networks or between a remote host and an access server. In this case, the IPv6 stations will make only limited use of the circuit switching capabilities of the network. They will be programmed to call a certain number when they are initialized to establish a circuit. Once the circuit is established, they will behave as if connected through a plain serial link.

However, some vendors are trying to push the use of ATM switches as a substitute for local networks, asserting that they provide faster transmission than classic Ethernet networks for a lesser price than FDDI or fast Ethernet technologies. Time and the market will tell us whether they are right. In between, we had to make sure that the neighbor discovery procedures also work in this environment, whose main characteristic is the absence of any multicast capability. We can indeed send a multicast IPv6 packet over an ATM circuit, but it will only reach the one station that is at the end of the circuit. In Internet jargon, we will say that ATM networks belong to the *nonbroadcast multiple access* category (NBMA). They provide connectivity between a large number of stations, but they do not provide multicast services.

To use IPv6 over such networks, the host should be configured with the ATM address (or X.25 address or more generally media address) of at least one router. It can then send router solicitations to this router or to all routers if it knows several addresses. It will receive router advertisements in responses, which will may be used for address autoconfiguration. Once it has configured its addresses, the host can inform the routers by sending unsolicited neighbor advertisement messages. The routers will keep track of the addresses of the connected hosts in their neighbors' caches.

In the absence of a multicast facility, the hosts will not be able to send neighbor solicitation messages. Whenever they must contact a new destination, they will simply consider that the next hop is their preferred router. If the destination is directly connected to the NBMA network, the router will send back a redirect message. The host will then update the destination cache, add an entry to the neighbors' cache, set up a circuit toward this new neighbor, and transmit the next packets over that new circuit.

4.3.3 Anycast Servers

An anycast address may be served by several stations connected to the same subnet. For example, one may assign an anycast address to "the world-wide-web server of the department," but replicate the service on three of the department's computers for better response time and resiliency. The anycast address of this service cannot be distinguished from a regular unicast address. It belongs to the department's subnet; it starts with the same prefix as the station's address.

All the stations that serve the anycast address will join the corresponding solicited-node multicast address. If a third party sends a neighbor solicitation toward that address, they will all reply by a neighbor advertisement. These advertisements will slightly differ from the regular neighbor advertisement, because the IPv6 source address will be the regular address of the station, not the anycast address. It would be illegal to use an anycast address as source address. The solicited bit, S, will not be set, because the source address is not equal to the target address.

The solicitor will receive several advertisements. The first will be used to complete the neighbors' cache entry corresponding to the anycast address. In theory, this first advertisement comes from the nearest or fastest of the anycast servers. The advertisement processing rules will guarantee that this first advertisement remains selected, as follows:

- When a host is waiting for an advertisement, when the neighbors' table entry is incomplete, the first advertisement is used to complete the table, even if the solicited bit is not set.

- When the neighbors' table entry is complete, advertisements whose solicited bit is not set are ignored. Advertisements with the solicited bit set may be received as part of the neighbor unreachability detection procedure. When solicited advertisements are received, the link layer address is updated.

The neighbor unreachability procedure will ensure that the binding to the current unicast address is quickly removed if the corresponding server fails.

4.3.4 Proxy servers

A subnetwork is identified by an address prefix or by a set of address prefixes. All stations whose addresses include this prefix are normally directly connected to the subnetwork. There are, however, some exceptions, when these stations are only accessible through a relay.

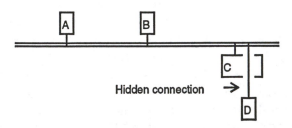

Hidden Connections Require Proxy Advertisements

This configuration is often used by mobility servers. When the mobile is docked in the office, it behaves as a regular host, such as A or B. When it is on the move, it keeps its address but asks for another station on the subnet to serve as a proxy, to receive the packets bound to its address and to relay them to its new position, using tunneling toward the new address.

In fact, the mobile may well ask several different stations to relay its packets in order to avoid relying on only one server. These stations must indeed synchronize their behavior, so that only one relays a given packet. The mechanisms are in fact exactly like those used by unicast servers.

4.3.5 Multihomed Hosts

Hosts that are connected to the network by several interfaces are said to be multihomed. Multihomed hosts are not routers. Their multiple connections are used for better performance and resiliency, but they are not expected to relay packets from one interface to the other. Not being routers, they do not participate in routing and do not have the knowledge of the network topology that routers acquire by running protocols such as RIP or OSPF.

When they have to transmit a packet toward a new destination, multihomed routers have to select an outgoing interface. They can use the prefix information received from routers on various interfaces to make the best choice when the destination happens to be a direct neighbor on one of their interfaces. If the destination address matches one of the interface's prefixes, then that interface will be selected.

When no prefix matches, the hosts have to make an arbitrary choice. They will probably pick the fastest interface or the interface where routers appears to be the most reliable.

4.3.6 Changing Interface Boards

In some cases the host knows that its link layer address has just changed, for example, after a "hot" replacement of an interface board. There is no need to reconfigure the IPv6 addresses at this stage, even if the unique token was derived from the old board's address. But the host may avoid temporary unreachability by multicasting an unsolicited neighbor advertisement message to the all nodes address. This message may be repeated a few times for better reliability.

4.4 Points of Controversy

The consensus on neighbor discovery procedures was only reached very recently. In between, we debated the model itself and the possibility of just using IPv4's ARP, the use of multicast addresses for neighbor solicitations, and the possibility of support mobility. We could even have tried to specify the autoconfiguration of routers.

4.4.1 Why Not Just ARP?

The original specification of SIP simply suggested the use of the IPv4 Address Resolution Protocol. There were some good reasons to keep the IPv4 model. In fact, the whole IPng effort has been an exercise in balancing between two options, the safe one, which would simply keep everything as much as possible like IPv4, and the brilliant one, which would try to take the opportunity of a white page to write the right thing.

Once the decision was taken to do an IPv6 specific discovery procedure, some suggested we use the ES-IS model of CLNP, in which end systems (hosts) do not take any routing decisions whatsoever, but always transmit the first packet for a new destination to an intermediate system (router). The routers are supposed to keep track of all the connected hosts and to send redirect messages if needed. This model was rejected because it places too much burden on the routers.

The neighbor discovery procedures, as they stand today, are in fact a reasonable compromise between the ARP and ES-IS extremes.

4.4.2 Broadcasting or Multicasting?

The neighbor discovery procedures rely heavily on multicasting. There are multicast addresses defined for the all nodes and all routers groups, as well as for the solicited-node multicast groups for all nodes whose addresses end with the same 32 bits. This use of a solicited-node multicast address raised some controversy, because of the relatively inefficient implementation of multicasting in many Ethernet boards.

When a node subscribes to a multicast group, it instructs its Ethernet board to accept the packets bound to the corresponding link-level multicast address. In theory, the Ethernet board could simply add the address to a list of selected multicast addresses and compare the incoming addresses to the elements of this list. But this would be slow or would require more hardware. Instead, most Ethernet chips compute a short hash code of the address and use it to index an array of bits. When a multicast address is selected, the corresponding bit is set. When a multicast packet arrives, the hash code of the address is computed. If the corresponding bit is set, the packet is accepted. If two multicast addresses result in the same hash code and if the node joins one of them, it will receive the packets from both groups. Indeed, this does not mean that the packets will be actually delivered to applications. The Ethernet drivers of the IPv6 drivers will silently discard the packets that were not desired. But this filtering will have to be done by software. The reception of the packet will trigger an interrupt that the computer will have to serve. It will steal some computer cycles, slowing down the normal applications. In mobile environments, it will wake up the portable unit, depleting the battery.

The problem is indeed that the most popular Ethernet components use a 6-bit hash code to index a 64-bit array. If more than 64 groups are active in the local subnet, we are bound to observe collisions. In the worst case, one of the station's solicited-node addresses will collide with the multicast address used by a videoconference application. This will generate hundreds of interrupts per second. This may very easily soak up all the computer cycles of an old personal computer or drain the battery of a small portable.

The alternative would be to use broadcasting instead of multicasting. But broadcasting has its own disadvantages. It means that all stations on the subnet are guaranteed to be awakened by all neighbor solicitations, even if they do have a modern Ethernet controller that uses either a large bit field or an explicit list of multicast groups. We have to choose here between the past, the old controllers, and the future, efficient implementation of multicasting. The group eventually chose the future. Old machines and their inefficient interfaces can always be relegated to specific subnets where no multimedia application is run.

4.4.3 Should We Support Mobility?

Many of us are convinced that the computers of the future will be mobile. They will be connected to the infrastructure through some form of wireless network, using microwave or infrared transmission.

Wireless networks are similar in many respects to Ethernet networks. In fact, the CSMA-CD protocol used by Ethernet networks is the natural evolution of protocols like ALOHA or CSMA that were first experimented with on radio channels. Wireless network generally allow multicast transmission. One could believe that the neighbor discovery procedures designed for plain multicast media would also be adequate for wireless media. This would be very short-sighted, because wireless transmission has some very specific constraints.

The quality of wireless transmissions depends on a number of parameters, such as the power of the emission, the quality and focus of the antenna and the distance between emitter and receiver. The transmission is not necessarily symmetric; a mobile station may well receive the powerful emissions of a fixed station, while this fixed station cannot understand the feeble signals of the mobile. The connectivity is also not necessarily transitive. It may well occur that A hears B, that B hears C, but that A does not hear C, for example when B lies between A and C. The neighbor discovery procedures include a number of parameters designed to facilitate the management of wireless media.

How much support would be needed for the wireless links was the subject of long disputes in the IETF working groups. The first versions of the neighbor discovery procedures included a *connectivity discovery* mechanism designed by William A. Simpson. The router advertisements and the neighbor advertisements would include the IPv6 addresses that the node had recently heard, together with an indication of quality. Bilateral connectivity between A and B would then be established if A's address was present in B's list of nodes heard and B's address present in A's list.

This procedure was removed in the final version of the document. We could not get a consensus that this was the right solution. Other solutions have been proposed, such as the mobile station would run a wireless specific routing protocol that could take advantage of any form of connectivity, even asymmetric.

4.4.4 Router Configuration

Designing an automatic address configuration procedure for hosts is a very good step forward, because the absence of this tool is currently slowing down the deployment of the Internet technology. But managers will still have to manually assign numbers to their various subnets. They will still have to configure these subnet numbers in their routers. We would very much like to give them automatic tools to also remove this burden.

The problem is indeed that these automatic tools have yet to be designed. This is not so much a point of controversy as a challenge for young network engineers!

4.5 Further Reading

The stateless autoconfiguration procedures are described in a draft document, "IPv6 Stateless Address Autoconfiguration," by Susan Thomson. This document should soon be published as an RFC.

The neighbor discovery procedures are described in a draft document, "Neighbor Discovery for IP Version 6 (IPv6)," by Thomas Narten, Erik Nordmark, and William A. Simpson. This document should soon be published as an RFC.

DHCP is defined by Ralph Droms in RFC 1541, "Dynamic Host Configuration Protocol," published in October 1993. A new version of this document is being prepared by the DHC working group of the IETF and should soon be published as an RFC. Jim Bound is currently preparing a document, "Dynamic Host Configuration Protocol for IPv6" that will also be published as an RFC.

The need to randomize timers is very well described in a communication by Van Jacobson and Sally Floyd to the 1993 Sigcomm symposium, "The Synchronisation of Periodic Routing Messages." The minutes of this symposium have been published in the October 1993 issue of the *ACM Computer Communication Review.*

Bringing Security
to the Internet

Hackers on the Internet have made press headlines more often than we would have liked. The attacks went in successive waves. Password cracking gave place to password sniffing, which was followed by the spoofing of addresses and the stealing of connections. There are great fears that organized criminals will follow the tracks of adventurous teenagers. Organizations are already beefing up their security, requesting the use of one-time passwords, and barricading their networks behind firewalls. There is some risk that all these security perimeters will end up balkanizing the Internet. To make a long story short, there is a great demand for security, and there was a big pressure on the IPv6 designers to incorporate serious security features in the new protocol. These security features will be a key incentive for transitioning to the new protocol. In fact, the result of this effort is the definition of IP-level authentication and encryption procedures that are common to IPv4 and IPv6. But the big difference is that they will have to be retrofitted into IPv4 implementations, whereas they will be present from day 1 in all IPv6 products.

5.1 Encryption and Authentication

The IPv6 specifications include the description of two security payloads, the *authentication header* and the *encrypted security payload*. One provides authentication, a procedure by which the recipient of a packet can guarantee that the source address is authentic and that the packet has not been altered during transmission. The other guarantees that only legitimate receivers will be able to read the content of the packet. Both are based on the concept of security association.

5.1.1 Security Association

Authentication and encryption require that senders and receivers agree on a key, on an authentication or encryption algorithm, and on a set of ancillary parameters such as the lifetime of the key or the details of the algorithm's utilization. This set of agreements constitutes a security association between the senders and the receivers. When packets are received, they can only be verified or decrypted if the receiver can link them with the context of a security association. The IPv6 authenticated and encrypted packets all convey a *security parameter index* (SPI).

When the packets are sent to a unique receiver through a unicast address, the SPI is chosen by this receiver. It may be, for example, the index into a table of security contexts maintained by this receiver. The SPI to use for each partner of a host will in fact be a parameter of the security association. Each station must remember the SPI used by its partner to identify the security context.

When the packets are sent to a group of receivers through a multicast address, the SPI is common to all members of the group. Each should be able to correlate the combination of group address and SPI with the key, algorithm, and other parameters information.

The SPI is normally negotiated as part of the key-exchange procedure.

5.1.2 Authentication Header

The *authentication header* (AH) is one of the generic extension headers that have been defined for IPv6. It is characterized by the payload type 51. It is typically inserted between the IPv6 header and the end-to-end payload. For example, an authenticated TCP packet will contain an IPv6 header, an authentication header, and the TCP packet itself. But several variations are possible, for example when a routing header is inserted before the AH or when end-to-end options are inserted between the AH and the payload.

The presence of the authentication header will not change the behavior of TCP, nor in fact of any other end-to-end protocol such as UDP or ICMP. It will simply provide explicit insurance for the origin

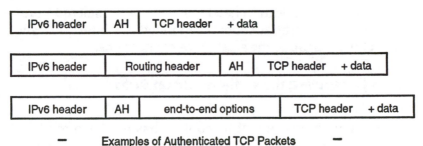

Examples of Authenticated TCP Packets

of the data. End-to-end protocols may indeed be instructed to reject any packets that would not be properly authenticated.

The authenticated header has a very simple syntax. It starts with a 64-bit header that comprises the number of the next header in the daisy chain, the length of the header in units of 32 bits, 16 reserved bits, which should be left to zero, and the 32-bit security parameter index of the security association. This fixed 64-bit header is followed by the authentication data, encoded as a variable number of 32-bit words.

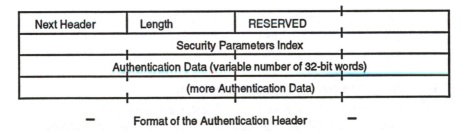

Format of the Authentication Header

The authentication data result from the computation of a cryptographic checksum, which involves the payload data, some fields of the IPv6 header and extension headers, and a secret shared by the members of the association. The precise length of the authentication data depends on the algorithm chosen to compute this checksum. The receiver will compute an expected value based on the content of the packet and the secret indexed by the SPI and will then compare the result of its computation with the authentication data received in the packet. If both values are equal, it can be ensured that the packet was formed by someone who knows the secret and that it was not modified in transit.

Use of the authentication header should be sufficient to prevent most address spoofing attacks observed in today's Internet. It should also protect users against the stealing of connections.

5.1.3 Computing the Authentication Data

The authentication header is designed to protect the integrity of the whole datagram, to check that its content has not been modified in transit. The problem, however, is that some fields have to be modified in transit. In the IPv6 header, the hop count is decremented at every hop. If the routing header is used, the IPv6 destination and the next address are swapped at every relay of the source route, while the next address is incremented. Some hop by hop options may also be updated in transit, as indicated by the *change en route* (C) bit of the option type.

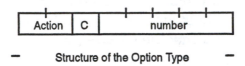

Structure of the Option Type

Before computing the authentication data, the sender must prepare a special version of the message, independent of transformations in transit:

- In the IPv6 header, the hop count is set to zero.
- If the routing header is used, the IPv6 destination is set to the final destination, the routing header content is set to the value that it should have upon arrival, and the address index will be set accordingly.
- Options whose C bit is set are not taken into account in the checksum computation. Their content is replaced by a set of zero bytes.

The checksum is then computed using a cryptographic algorithm. Conventional checksum algorithms such as the classic IP 16-bit checksum or the 16- or 32-bit polynomial checksums used in serial links and Ethernet networks should not be used here. Anyone who has a sufficient knowledge of mathematics will understand that these algorithms are far too weak. It is trivial to tweak some bits in the messages so that the classic checksum remains unchanged. It is even feasible to reverse engineer the checksum and discover the secret part. In short, these algorithms are designed to protect messages against random errors caused by noise in the lines, not against determined offenders.

The algorithm suggested in the IP security architecture is known as *keyed MD5*. It is derived from the message digest 5 algorithm, MD5, designed by Ronald Rivest. MD5 computes a 128-bit checksum of the message, or rather a 128-bit hash code, using nonlinear transformations that make reverse engineering extremely difficult, although not entirely impossible given a lot of time and millions of dollars of budget. Keyed MD5 operates by combining the message with a secret key and then computing the hash code on the result. The key is both prepended and appended to the message in order to prevent certain types of attacks. The exact sequence of operation is the following:

1. *Obtain a transmission-independent version M' of the message M by zeroing the hop count and then changing options and forming the final destination version of the routing header,*

2. *As MD5 operates on blocks of 16 octets, pad M' with null bytes to the next 16-octet boundary. The secret key K should also be padded with null bytes to the next 16-octet boundary.*

3. *Compute the MD5 hash code of a message obtained by concatenating K, M', and again K.*

The authentication algorithm is in fact negotiated as part of the establishment of the security association. The MD5 algorithm is only specified as a default to make sure that all implementations can at least use one common algorithm. One can reasonably expect that other algorithms will also be used in the future, algorithms thst would be either faster to compute or harder to crack than MD5.

5.1.4 Encrypted Security Payload

The authentication header does not transform the data. They remain in the clear, subject for example to sniffers' attacks. When confidentiality is desired, the *encrypted security payload* should be used. This header is always the last one in the daisy chain of IPv6 extension headers. More precisely, it is the last one that remains visible once encryption is applied.

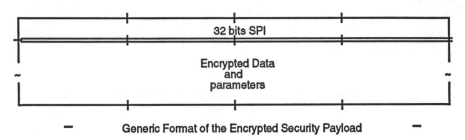

An Encrypted Packet Using the ESP Header

In fact, the ESP header has been designed so that only the security parameter index remains in clear-text. Other parameters, such as
the payload type of the encrypted data, are encrypted together with
the data.

| 32 bits SPI |
| Encrypted Data and parameters |

Generic Format of the Encrypted Security Payload

The precise format depends in fact on the particular encryption
algorithm that is being used. The default algorithm suggested by the
specification is the cipher block chaining mode of the Data Encryption Standard (DES-CBC). When DES-CBC is used, the encrypted
data start with a variable-length *initialization vector*, followed by the
encrypted value of the payload itself, some padding octets, a padding length indicator, and the payload type.

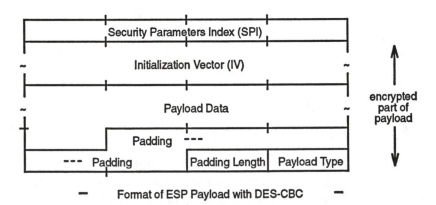

Format of ESP Payload with DES-CBC

The length of the padding is chosen so that the message ends on
a 64-bit word boundary. The padding octets may have any value.

The last octet in the decrypted message indicates the type of payload, for example TCP. The previous octet indicates the number of padding bytes.

The *initialization vector* (IV) is composed of a variable number of 32-bit words. The precise number is defined as a parameter of the security association. The content of the IV is normally the result of a random number generator. The role of the IV is to ensure that the first words of the messages cannot be predicted, that the hackers cannot use methods based on the knowledge of both the clear-text and the encrypted value. This randomness is propagated to the remaining words of the message by the cipher block chaining algorithm.

As for MD5 in the case of authentication, DES-CBC is only a default algorithm. Other algorithms can be selected when the security association is being established.

5.1.5 Authentication and Confidentiality

Authentication and confidentiality are two different services. One guarantees that the message comes from the right origin and has not been altered; the other guarantees that the message cannot be listened to by third parties. Most encryption methods provide some indication of the message origin. Encryption algorithms are rather good at generating random bits when the message is not encrypted or decrypted with the right key, so a few semantic checks suffice to decide whether the encryption was successful. This is not, however, a complete guarantee. Some subtle attacks can be performed by combining fragments of previously encoded messages so that the result of the decryption "looks right," although it is not authentic.

When both strong authentication and confidentiality are requested, it is possible to combine the two payloads, either by inserting an authentication header before the ESP or by encrypting a message composed of the authentication header and the actual payload. Other methods can also be used, such as choosing a security transform that includes a cryptographic checksum in the encrypted data.

5.2 Key Distribution

The establishment of security associations relies on the existence of secret keys known only to the members of the association. Efficient deployment of security will rely on the existence of an efficient key distribution method. The link between the key management and the security protocols is indeed the security parameter index of the security association. The key management procedures are expected to not only provide the keys, but also the other parameters of the security association.

The Internet community has yet to agree on a key distribution method. The leading proposal is called Photuris and is based on zero knowledge exchanges, completed by authentication of the exchanging parties. In the absence of an agreed on mechanism, early deployments are likely to rely on manual key distribution. A special case will be that of multicast groups, which require special algorithms.

5.2.1 The Design of Photuris

The Photuris proposal is based on the zero-knowledge key exchange algorithm proposed by Whitfield Diffie and Martin Hellman. In the original Diffie –Hellman proposal, the two parties, A and B, agree on a prime number p and a generator g. The party A will then pick a random number x. It will compute the value

$$n = g^x \bmod p$$

and transmit it to B. B, in turn, will pick a random number y, compute the valuero

$$m = g^y \bmod p$$

and transmit it to A. At this stage, A knows m and x, B knows n and y while third parties may know m or n, but cannot obtain either x or y. A and B can compute the session key:

$$z = n^y \bmod p = m^x \bmod p = g^{xy} \bmod p$$

This key could then be used by encryption or the authentication algorithm. The Diffie–Hellman exchange can be implemented with other mathematical techniques, such as elliptic curve groups.

Using zero-knowledge exchanges for IP security has at least two advantages:

■ Keys are computed when needed. There is no need to keep values secret for long periods. Experience shows that it is difficult to keep a secret very long in a computer.

■ The exchange does not require any preexisting infrastructure such as key servers or certificate servers. It can thus be very easily deployed.

The original Diffie–Hellman algorithm has, however, a set of known weaknesses:

■ It does not provide any information about the identities of the parties.

■ It is subject to the *man-in-the-middle attack*, by which a third party C postures as B for A and A for B. Both A and B end up negotiating a key with C, which can then listen to their traffic.

■ It involves heavy computation. The algorithm is only safe when p is a large prime number, say a thousand bits long. The duration of a single multiplication varies as the square of the size of p; the number of multiplications required by an exponentiation varies with the number of bits of the exponent.

■ The heavy computational load can be used in a clogging attack, in which the opponent requests a high number of keys. The victim spends all its computing power doing useless exponentiation instead of real work.

The design of Photuris tries to keep the advantages of the Diffie–Hellman algorithm while addressing its weaknesses:

■ Photuris supports a variety of authentication methods that can be coupled with the key exchange. Adequate authentication will prevent the man-in-the-middle attack.

■ Photuris uses a set of predefined primes. This avoids the long computation required to discover long prime numbers and also enables stations to choose random half-keys and to compute the corresponding exponentiation in advance.

■ In Photuris, the Diffie–Hellman algorithm is preceded by a cookie exchange. This will either thwart the clogging attack or at a minimum oblige the saboteurs to disclose their Internet address.

The algorithm name is not an acronym, but rather a tribute to some unknown engineers. Photuris is the Greek name used by zoologists to designate the firefly. Firefly, in turn, is the name of the classified key exchange designed by NSA for the STU-III secure telephone. A rumor tells us that the design of Photuris is very close to that of the NSA's Firefly. It may well just be an urban legend. The author of this book, being a French citizen, has absolutely no way to verify this information.

5.2.2 Photuris Exchanges

The Photuris protocol starts by a cookie exchange, followed by a Diffie–Hellman exchange. Once the Diffie–Hellman computation is completed and the keys installed, signature messages are sent over the protected channels.

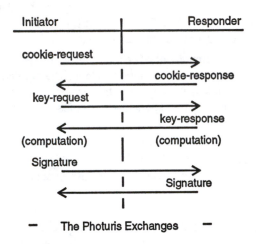

— The Photuris Exchanges —

All Photuris messages are exchanged over UDP. On each station, the Photuris server awaits request on UDP port 468.

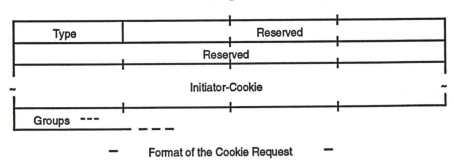

— Format of the Cookie Request —

The cookie request is identified by the message type 0. It contains a 128-bit *initiator cookie*, a random number chosen by the initiator to identify that exchange. It also contains a list of groups, the word group being used here according to the mathematical theory to designate a number space where the Diffie–Hellman computations may take place. Each group is identified by an 8-bit number. The current draft supplies three groups, identified by their numbers:

- Number 1 is an elliptic curve group.
- Number 2 is an exponential group based on a 1024-bit prime number. The generator is the number 2.
- Number 5 is another exponential group based on another 1024-bit prime number. The generator is the number 5.

Implementations may define other numbers. All implementations will support the group number 2.

When a Photuris responder receives a cookie request, it examines the list of groups provided by the requestor and selects one. It will then compute a *responder cookie*, typically by applying a cryptographic one-way function such as MD5 to a string composed of the source address and UDP port of the message, the initiator cookie, and a secret number drawn by the responder when it was initialized. The responder will then compose a response message and send it to the initiator. It will not normally keep any memory of the exchange.

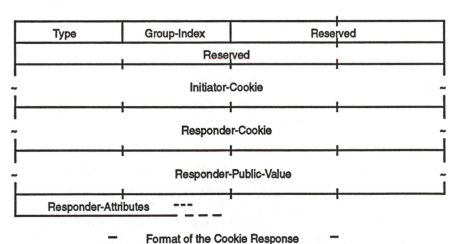

Format of the Cookie Response

The cookie response is identified by the message type 1. The message contains a group index, selected from the list of groups provided by the initiator, a copy of the initiator cookie, a responder cookie, a responder public value, and a list of attributes. The responder cookie is a semirandom number that identifies the exchange for the responder. The responder public value is a variable precision number whose exact format depends on the selected group. The list of attributes contains a set of transforms, in order of responder preference. Attributes are identified by an 8-bit type number. Types have been defined for a plethora of transforms.

0	padding
1	unassigned
2	MD2
3	unassigned
4	MD4
5	MD5
6	MD6 (reserved)
7	RSA
8	PGP certificate
9	X.509 certificate
10	DNS-SIG certificate
11	unassigned
12	RC2
13	unassigned
14	RC4
15	unassigned
16	DES-CBC, 0-bit IV
17	DES-CBC, 32-bit IV
18	DES-CBC, 64-bit IV
19	unassigned
20	Triple DES-CBC, 0-bit IV
21	Triple DES-CBC, 32-bit IV
22	Triple DES-CBC, 64-bit IV
23	unassigned
24	SHA
25	DSS
26	IDEA
27	LZ77
28	Stac LZS
29-254	unassigned
255	Administratively Configured

List of Transforms Defined in Photuris

Codes have been assigned to several one-way functions that can be used in the AH (MD4, MD5, SHA) to several encryption procedures that can be used in the ESP, such as DES-CBC or triple DES, a variation of DES that uses twice longer keys and is much stronger. In the case of DES and triple DES, different code points have been assigned to three different initialization vector lengths, 0, 32, and 64 bits. Codes have also been assigned to some compression functions, notably LZ77 and Stac LZS, and to some signature methods, notably RSA public keys or their embedding in various forms of certificates as defined by the PGP software, the X.509 standard of the ITU, or the secure version of the Domain Name System. Attributes are encoded as a type-length-value sequence, although in most cases there is no value field, the only exceptions being some compression algorithms. Public keys and certificates used by signatures will be transmitted later, during the signature exchange.

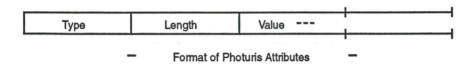

—   Format of Photuris Attributes   —

The *initiator cookie* is used by the initiator to correlate the request and the response. Initiators are supposed to associate a timer with each exchange. If the response does not arrive in due time, the procedure will be retried. It should, however, be retried with a different initiator cookie, because the responder may very well keep copies of the recently received requests and refuse to serve them more than once, in an attempt to thwart certain forms of sabotage. Saturated receivers may also elect to ignore incoming cookie requests, for example, if too many security associations are active at the same time.

Once it has received the cookie response, the initiator chooses a half-key and the corresponding public value in the indexed group, the number space chosen by the responder. It also chooses the attributes that will be used in the security association in the initiator-to-responder direction and sends a key request message.

The *key request* indicates the SPI that will be used in the responder-to-initiator direction and the lifetime of this association. The group index, initiator cookie, and responder cookie are copied from the cookie response message. The initiator public value is a variable precision integer, encoded as a 16-bit length field followed by the necessary number of octets. The *initiator transform* parameter indicates the transforms chosen by the initiator in the responder's list, encoded as a 16-bit length field followed by a list of 8-bit attribute numbers. The message is completed by the initiator list of attributes.

When it receives a key request message, the responder first checks the validity of the responder cookie. Messages whose cookie is incorrect are simply ignored. If the message is acceptable, the responder chooses its own half of the key, as well as a set of transforms from the initiator's attribute list and a key transform that will

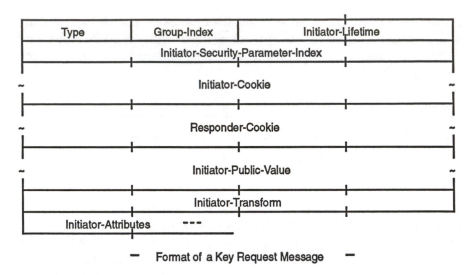

— Format of a Key Request Message —

be used in the exchange of signatures. These parameters are sent in the key-response message.

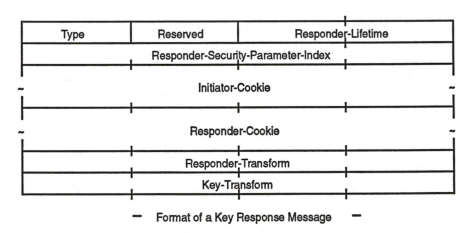

— Format of a Key Response Message —

The key response message also contains the SPI of the association in the direction from responder to initiator. The session keys can be computed immediately after the exchange of half-keys. The session key will be formally composed of the D–H shared-secret, concatenated with the SPI, the SPI owner cookie, and the peer cookie. The actual key will then be shortened by applying a one-way function such as MD5 to this string to obtain a set of 128 bits used in the security association. The particular hash function that will be used is chosen from the initiator's list of attributes and indicated in the key transform parameter. A different key will be used in each direction.

The lifetime of the association is chosen by the responder. Lifetimes are typically rather short, for example 30 seconds. Long lifetimes increase the risk of compromising the key. It is preferable to reinitiate the association and to compute new keys. These repetitions may, however, use the same public components as the initial exchange, so stations may remember the public components and expedite the computation. The use of a key transform will guarantee that a different key will be used for each association.

The key exchange is protected by a timer. If the initiator does not receive a key response in due time, it will repeat the request. The responders keep a copy of recently received requests and detect duplicate messages. In this case, they will just repeat their response. The parties may also use a key change indication to set up the new key.

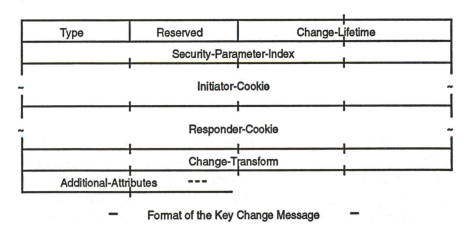

Format of the Key Change Message

The *key change message* is used to derive a new association, with a new SPI, from an existing one. The key is obtained by applying a transform, selected from the partner's list of attributes, to the previous key.

5.2.3 Authenticating the Keys

The cookie exchange and the Diffie–Hellman exchange do not provide any identification of receiver and initiator, besides the simple fact that both can receive and transmit messages from their Internet address. Once this exchange has been completed, the security associations are established. They can be used to exchange signatures in order to check the identities of the initiator and receiver, as well as for the absence of a man in the middle.

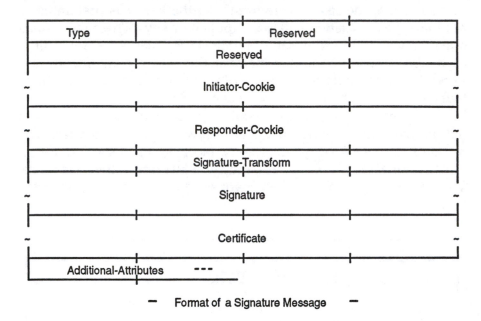

| Type | Reserved | |
| Reserved | | |
| ~ Initiator-Cookie ~ |
| ~ Responder-Cookie ~ |
| Signature-Transform |
| ~ Signature ~ |
| ~ Certificate ~ |
| Additional-Attributes - - - |

— Format of a Signature Message —

The *signature request message* is sent by the initiator over the secure association that has just been installed. The message contains the initiator and receiver cookies, an electronic signature, the certificates used for that signature, and some additional attributes. The signature transforms will typically consist of a one-way function followed by an RSA exponentiation with the private key of the initiator. The particular one-way function and public key exponentiation method, as well as the type of certificates used to validate the public key, are chosen from the responder's list of attributes.

The transform is applied to a string made of the session key, concatenated with the initiator's public value, the responder's public value, and optionally the identifying public key, certificate, or distinguishing name of the sender. Inclusion of the public values in the string guarantees that a man in the middle has not substituted its own value. If the verification succeeds, the responder computes its own signature and sends it to the initiator. If it fails, an error message is sent and the security association is dropped.

5.2.4 Manual Key Distribution

The Photuris procedures allow stations to set up security association, specifying an SPI and a list of authentication, encryption, and compression transforms in each direction, as well as an association's lifetime. Manual distribution can indeed achieve the same result, albeit with larger expense for personnel.

Implementations of IP security should allow operators to manually set up associations.

5.2.5 Key Distribution for Multicast Groups

Multicast groups pose a difficult problem because all members of the group must obtain the same key. The Photuris algorithm is not very useful there, because the use of Diffie–Hellman exchanges completed by a key transform results in the selection of a random value. The distribution of group keys will have to rely on a key server. It is, however, perfectly reasonable to use Photuris to set up secure associations between the group members and the group's key servers.

5.3 Usage of IPv6 Security

There are multiple potential usages of IPv6 security, notably between firewalls, between mobile hosts and their bases, and between secure hosts. The authentication procedure may be very useful to protect networking procedures such as neighbor discovery or the exchange of routing information.

5.3.1 Steel Pipes and Firewalls

Current implementations of Internet security rely largely on the use of firewalls, secure machines that act as a gateway between the secure premises of the organization and the cruel world outside. IPv6 AH and ESP can be used to establish a secure tunnel between two distant firewalls, for example between two units of the same organization.

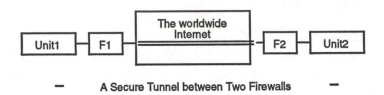

— A Secure Tunnel between Two Firewalls —

The packet exchanges between the two units will be encapsulated into IPv6 packets transmitted from one firewall to the other through the worldwide Internet, using either the AH if only authentication is requested or the ESP if confidentiality is needed. Supposing that authentication is used, a typical packet exchanged between the station U1 in unit 1 and the station U2 in unit 2 will undergo two successive transforms at the firewalls F1 and F2:

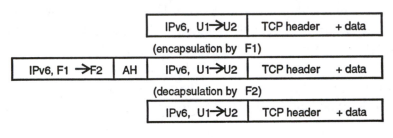

— Encapsulation and Decapsulation —

The secure tunnel between the two locations can be thought of as a steel pipe that protects the exchanges. If authentication is used, opponents cannot inject spoofed packets. If encryption is used, they cannot see through the pipe.

5.3.2 Mobile Hosts

Mobile hosts are an important concern for security-conscious organizations. The mobile will be plugged into all sorts of remote networks on which the organizations' managers have little control

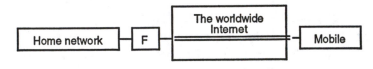

— A Secure Tunnel between a Mobile Unit and a Firewall —

One very easy way to fend off the specific attacks on mobile computers is to establish a secure tunnel between the mobile unit and the home network's firewall. This solution may be combined with the implementation of IP-level mobility if the firewall acts as the home base for the mobile and acts as a proxy for that mobile in the neighbor discovery procedure. The mobile will then have two addresses, one in the distant network and one in the home network. Packets bound to his home address will be relayed by the firewall using secure encapsulation.

5.3.3 Secure Hosts

Firewalls and mobile servers are network objects whose installation is transparent to most applications. The payload type of the header following the H or the ESP will always indicate the presence of an IPv6 packet. Secure applications will be aware of the existence of IP security. They may request to only receive authenticated packets, or to only send encrypted packets. In this case, the type of the payload following the AH or the ESP will typically be TCP or UDP.

The deployment of this service supposes extensions to the network programming interfaces, such as sockets, to incorporate the new requests. These extensions will be present from the beginning in IPv6 implementations.

5.3.4 Neighbor Discovery

Some networking procedures have specific security requirements. Neighbor discovery is a good example. We would very much like to control the access to our networks so that visitors could only plug in their portable computers if they are explicitly authorized to do so. We would also very much like to control the authenticity of some messages, so that our stations do not end up sending data to the wrong address. In particular, we would like to check that

- Router advertisements come from an authorized router
- Neighbor advertisements come from an authorized station
- Redirect messages come from the router to which the initial packet was sent

Router advertisements are sent to the all nodes multicast group. One could easily configure a secure association for that group, defined by a SPI, an algorithm such as MD5, and a session key. One should, however, notice that symmetric algorithms such as MD5 can only protect the group from outsiders. Because the key is known to all stations in the group, each can posture as a router. But this is much better than the current situation in which any hacker can branch a computer to the local network.

Neighbor advertisements are sent to the unicast address of the solicitor. They can only be secured if a security association has been established between the neighbor and the solicitor, which somehow poses a chicken and egg problem. How can they negotiate a key if they have not yet exchanged a packet? There are two solutions to this dilemma. The network manager may let the stations negotiate a security association at a later stage. It may also program the routers not to advertise the local prefixes, forcing hosts to always pick a router as their first next hop and to rely on authenticated redirects for local communications.

Securing the exchanges between routers and hosts is much easier, because each host only communicates with a small number of routers. Hosts may very well set up secure associations with the local routers or at the very least with their preferred router. The only problem here is that of authentication, which requires hosts to use a pair of public and private keys. This is hardly compatible with the dentist's office or thousand computers on the dock constraints.

5.3.5 Routing Protocols

Network integrity cannot be maintained if routing protocols are not secured. If intruders may forge routing updates, they will be able to disrupt the communication or divert some connections. Protocols such as RIP, OSPF, or IDRP should be run on top of security associations between the routers. Using IP security is probably a good alternative to the definition of protocol-specific authentication or encryption functions.

5.4 Points of Controversy

The definition of security for IPv6 generated some heated debates. In principle, nobody opposes the addition of security functions to the Internet protocol. However, when these functions were eventually defined as a mandatory part of the new Internet Protocol, three questions were raised:

- Encryption is plagued with patents and export control restrictions. Should we really make its implementation mandatory for conformance?
- To guarantee interoperability, the specifications mandate the implementation of MD5 for authentication and DES-CBC for encryption. Are we sure that these are the correct algorithms?
- The specifications specify that authentication and encryption are implemented as Internet layer functions. Is this the correct layer?

These debates were among the worst that I ever observed in the IETF. It seems that everything related to security is bound to generate an incredible amount of heat, not to mention some foul play.

5.4.1 Should We Mandate Security?

The use of encryption protocols has long been reserved to armies and secret services. Securing communication lines is essential to efficient military actions. Conversely, attacking the enemies' communications is a good way to increase your own efficiency. The example of the German Enigma machine, which British intelligence was able to crack during World War II, is still fresh in our memories. It follows that governments would prefer not to observe the development of a worldwide free trade of encryption products that could be bought and used by unfriendly forces, terrorist organizations, and organized crime.

Most countries impose export restrictions in this domain. Exporting encryption products requires special licenses. These licenses are often negotiated on a case by case basis. Rumor says that U.S. licenses are only granted to products whose codes the NSA can crack. Some countries, like Iraq or France, are even more restrictive. In addition to export, they also regulate domestic usage so that the police forces can easily listen to private communications. Some U.S. federal agencies tried to regulate encryption and impose the use of the "Clipper chip" for precisely that reason. The chip had a "back door" that they could use to easily break the codes.

Manufacturers suffer from these restrictions. If they develop a product that offers strong security for the U.S. market, they will have to develop a watered down version for export. In practice, this means two products instead of one, twice the documentation and maintenance effort. They have long been lobbying for an easing of the export restrictions, but their efforts have not yet been successful, even if the efficiency of the restrictions is quite questionable. The mathematical theory of encryption is well known, books are available that detail the algorithms, and any good engineer can develop a product based on these books. There are good engineers in all industrialized or semiindustrialized countries, and some pretty good software encryption products have indeed been available on the Internet for many years. Everybody believes that we are in fact witnessing the last-ditch battle of the governments, that they will not be able to cling much longer to their privileges and that the rights of citizens to privacy will eventually prevail. But computer companies are not civil rights activists. They have to obey the regulations and cannot in practice develop an IPv6 conformant product in the United States and export it worldwide.

Their situation would probably have been easier if the availability of the ESP and DES-CBC algorithms had not been made an integral part of the IPv6 specification. They would simply have developed the authentication header, which can be exported without many problems. Encryption support would have been an additional product that could be bought from special providers. But the IETF consensus was that this would not be good enough. There was fear that if encryption was not mandated in the specification it would simply not be implemented. There was also a strong desire to send a forceful message to the community. Encryption is the only way to deter sniffing attacks on passwords or credit card numbers. It is absolutely necessary to implement it if we want to develop commercial usage of the Internet.

There are in fact many possibilities for the manufacturers. Few countries, besides Iraq and France, regulate import. One could thus select to develop the encryption products in a country such as Finland or Switzerland, which do not regulate exports, assemble the IPv6 package there, and export it from this neutral country to the whole world. Alternatively, one could ask developers in each country to produce a national version of ESP and DES-CBC, integrate it locally with the IPv6 product, and distribute it nationally. We may well foresee that once encryption products have become a commodity in a sufficient number of countries the export controls will be gradually eased or dropped.

5.4.2 Did We Choose the Correct Algorithm?

Once the decision was taken to actually standardize IP security, we observed a surprising attack by security experts on the particulars of that decision. The algorithms we picked were, according to them, either not secure enough or too slow, or maybe both.

The MD5 algorithm computes a 128-bit hash code from a message of arbitrary length. In theory, one would need 2 to the power 128 trials before finding a new message that results in the same MD5 hash. Even if each trial only lasted a nanosecond, this would require some billions of billions of centuries. But recent advances in cryptography have shown that one could take advantage of the particularities of the algorithm and speed up the process. According to Paul C. van Oorschot and Michael J. Wiener, one could build a machine that could find messages that match an arbitrary MD5 hash. The machines would cost about $10 million and it would take about 24 days to find one checksum. This does indeed mean that decryption technology is catching up and that a 128-bit hash code will soon not be sufficient. However, MD5 will remain a valid one-way function for quite some time.

Similar observations could be made against DES-CBC. The DES uses only a 56-bit key. One can probably design custom VLSI that would perform a billion DES encryptions per second. One could then build a parallel machine with a million of these components and break any DES key in about three days. These figures suppose an exhaustive search. If the clear-text is known or if one can use differential analyses, the search for the key would be even faster. The general consensus is that the DES is still a good code for routine encryptions but that its key is too short for protecting "really secret" transactions.

The arguments about the speed of the algorithms are also well founded. The fastest implementations of MD5 on a high-speed RISC processor showed that the algorithm could compute hash codes at about 60 megabits per second. This is already a bit slow for fast Ethernets or FDDI rings and entirely inadequate for HIPPI or Myrinet networks, which deliver up to 650 Mbps. DES is even slower. The algorithm was designed for hardware implementations. The fastest software implementations, on modern RISC processors, run at about 10 Mbps.

But, then, there are few other choices. MD5 and DES-CBC were chosen because they were very well known and largely available. They are already used in secure versions of some routing protocols, or in the version 2 of the Simple Network Management Protocol. There are some alternatives, but they are either weaker or slower than MD5 and DES-CBC. The speed of computation problem was well noted, but it is inherent to any serious cryptographic algorithm that attempts to hide data by a set of computations. Again, there was a feeling that, if we did not mandate at least one algorithm for each function, then the tower of Babel effect would prevail and no inter-operation would be possible.

One should also observe that the key management protocol does provide the opportunity to negotiate other algorithms. Codes have been allocated to SHA, a one-way function that computes 160-bit hash codes and is supposedly stronger than MD5, or to the Triple-DES whose keys are twice longer than those of the simple DES. If these algorithms provide added value over MD5 and DES-CBC, the market will adopt them and they will become the default algorithms in a few years, when the protocols are revised. In between, it is important to proceed to deploy some reasonable solution. Nothing could be worse than the current absence of security.

5.4.3 Is This the Right Layer?

The AH and ESP security payloads provide an Internet-level service. There was a strong consensus among network specialists that this was just right. There was also a strong dissent among the developers of applications. The problem is one of development cost versus deployment cost.

If security is provided at the Internet level, it becomes a stan-dard service that all applications can use. The development of secure application is made simpler. It is even possible to add security trans-parently to existing applications if the Internet protocol software is upgraded. It suffices to instruct the operating system to always set up a security association before starting a TCP connection or a UDP exchange.

But the deployment of Internet-level security presupposes the deployment of a new network code. Application developers are often reluctant to rely on the specificities of the platform on which their applications run. They are used to developing codes that would work on PCs as well as Macintoshes or UNIX workstations. They will only use one specific feature if it is available on all the platforms. Otherwise, they would have to develop emulation code for those systems where the facility is not available or accept selling a software with reduced capabilities. On the other hand, if they incorporate the function in the application program, they can guarantee its availabil-ity to all their clients.

The developers of IPv6 have three responses to the application developers' arguments. First, because security is an integral part of IPv6, it will be available on all platforms. Second, the complexity of security algorithms is such that there is a real advantage in using an externally provided component. Third, some attacks can only be thwarted by Internet-level security. This is notably the case of denial of service attacks on TCP connections. An intruder who can listen to ongoing conversations is capable of forging Reset commands that will interrupt the TCP connection, even if its content is encrypted by the application. These attacks will be fended off it the TCP headers are authenticated or encrypted.

5.4.4 Do We Need Additional Protection?

The IP-level mechanisms that are included in the IPv6 specifications will provide a dramatic improvement in the security of the Internet. Some further developments will, however, be needed if we want protection against traffic analysis or denial or service attacks.

Spies and hackers could obtain a lot of useful information by just watching the pattern of traffic that is flowing over the Internet, counting the packets and drawing a matrix of traffic. An obvious protection against these attacks is to ask providers to secure their networks, but customers cannot always trust the providers. Communications may cross several providers' networks, maybe in several countries. The users may try to disguise their traffic by the use of tunnels, relaying the packets through trusted third parties, which will build up an opaque overlay network on top of the Internet. They may also inject some random traffic in order to flatten the matrix, to add a sufficient level of noise to the signals that the spies may obtain. We have very little experience with these techniques.

Denials of service attacks can be performed by sending random traffic to a set of specific destinations, saturating the access line of a particular user. This recently occurred to a couple of Arizona lawyers who had swamped the Internet news service with their advertisements. Angry internauts retaliated by bombing them with mail messages containing very long binary attachments. Very soon, their links were so saturated that they could not use their connection anymore. In fact, the whole regional network was congested. The same attacks could well be conducted by pressure groups, religious organizations or hysterical ecology movements against government administrations, research institutions, or manufacturing companies.

Protection against these attacks requires that the intermediate routers reserve some capacity to legitimate users, checking the source and destination addresses. But source addresses can be forged, and real protection requires that the intermediate routers check the origin of the addresses, perhaps by using some version of the authentication header.

Nobody should believe that security will just arrive because we specified a couple of protocols. More work, more research, more experience are needed. On the other hand, the standardization of encryption, authentication, and key management is certainly a big step forward!

5.5 Further Reading

The IP security functions are defined by a set of five RFCs: "Security Architecture for the Internet Protocol" by Ran Atkinson (RFC 1825), "IP Authentication Header" by Ran Atkinson (RFC 1826), "IP Authentication Using Keyed MD5" by Perry Metzger and William A. Simpson (RFC 1828), "IP Encapsulating Security Payload (ESP)" by Ran Atkinson (RFC 1827), and "The ESP DES-CBC Transform" by Perry Metzger, Phil Karn, and William A. Simpson (RFC 1829).

RFC 1321, "The MD5 Message-Digest Algorithm," by Ronald Rivest, was published in April 1992. The possible attack on MD5 by special-purpose hardware was described by Paul C. van Oorschot and Michael J. Wiener in "Parallel Collision Search with Application to Hash Functions and Discrete Logarithms," a communication to the 2nd ACM Conference on Computer and Communications Security, held at Fairfax, Virginia, in November 1994.

The "Data Encryption Standard" was first published in January 1977 by the U.S. National Bureau of Standards as Federal Information Processing Standard (FIPS) Publication 46. The Cipher Block Chaining is one of the "Data Encryption Standard Modes of Operation" published in December 1980 as Federal Information Processing Standard (FIPS) Publication 81. The U.S. National Bureau of Standards also published "Guidelines for Implementing and Using the Data Encryption Standard" as Federal Information Processing Standard (FIPS) Publication 74 in April 1981, and republished the "Data Encryption Standard" as Federal Information Processing Standard (FIPS) Publication 46-1 in January 1988.

Photuris is described in a draft, "The Photuris Session Key Management Protocol," by Phil Karn and William A. Simpson. This draft will probably be revised before being published as an RFC.

The discussion of denial of service attacks can be found in RFC 1636, "Report of the IAB Workshop on Security in the Internet Architecture—February 8–10, 1994."

On the general subject of cryptography, recommended reading is Bruce Schneier's book *Applied Cryptography*, published by John Wiley & Sons, Inc.

6

Real-time Support
and Flows

The very first draft of the SIP protocol was published by Steve Deering in the fall of 1992. One initial assumption of SIP was alignment on 64-bit boundaries. The initial version comprised two 64-bit addresses for source and destination and some ancillary fields such as packet length, payload type, or hop count. These ancillary fields did not, however, require 64 bits, and Steve was left with about 32 extra bits. He polled various experts on the best use of these bits. Some wanted to insert a checksum; others wished for longer length or hop count fields. The most convincing requirement, however, was for a flow identifier that could be used to identify real-time flows, to allocate resources and priorities through some reservation protocol. A proper handling of flows was required if we wanted to provide high-quality multimedia communications in the new Internet. Steve followed the advice. After more than two years of discussions and refinements, this resulted in the definitions of the flow label and priority class of IPv6.

6.1 An Elusive Specification

The IPv6 specification does define flows. This definition, however, is carefully worded not to imply any specific property. "A flow is a sequence of packets sent from a particular source to a particular (unicast or multicast) destination for which the source desires special handling by the intervening routers." In fact, the definition of flow comes implicitly from the definition of flow label itself. A flow is the set of packets that comes from the same source to the same destination and bears the same flow label. In this section, we will see how flows relate with priorities, with exception routing, and with setup procedures.

6.1.1 Defining Flow Labels and Priorities

The set of packets that constitutes a flow is identified by a 24-bit flow label. There is no requirement that all packets belong to flows. In fact, it is very likely that during a transition period most packets will not be explicitly labeled as belonging to flows. The data will be generated by classic applications programs such as SMTP mailers, FTP file transfers or HTTP web browsers. These programs have been designed for IPv4 and will be upgraded to handle both IPv4 and IPv6 addresses, but will probably not be modified to incorporate a flow handling procedure that IPv4 would not support. The corresponding packets will use a null flow label, composed of 24 zero bits.

Flow labels will be used when the transmission mandates some special treatment, for example, for applications with severe real-time constraints.

6.1.2 Flows and Policy Routes

The flow label may be used in conjunction with the routing header. In fact, one could very well assume that all packets that are explicitly source routed through the same set of relays "require a specific processing." This does not imply that all packets routed on the same source route belong to the same application: they may belong to different video streams, or to a mix of audio, video, and data streams.

Multimedia communications can last for a relatively long time. Source routing requirements may well change during that time. It may well be that a secondary provider of connectivity offers better tariffs than the organization's primary provider during certain times of the day. Customers who want to take advantage of these tariffs will, for example, use standard routing until 1 P.M. and then insert a routing header to force secondary routing between 1 P.M. and 2 P.M. From an application point of view, the packets belong to the same flow. But the specifications are quite clear: if the source routing changes, the flow label must also change. In our example, the packets transmitted between 1 P.M. and 2 P.M. will have to bear a different label than those transmitted before 1 P.M. or after 2 P.M.

6.1.3 Flows, Not Virtual Circuits

At a time when the old virtual circuits mechanism of X.25 revive in ATM, it is tempting to equate IPv6 flows with the virtual circuits that telephone operators so much praised. This would be a mistake. The routing of IPv6 packets can only be influenced by a judicious choice of the destination address or by the insertion of a routing header. The labeling of flow does not have any effect on the routing. In fact, the designers of IPv6 could easily explain why they believe that ATM is "a serious mistake." But this is not the purpose of this book.

6.2 Supporting Reservations

Most experts who recommended the addition of a flow label to the basic IPv6 header had resource reservation in mind. They had observed that traditional packet switching did not support well the hard real-time applications such as voice or video transfers. They thought that resource reservation was a necessary enhancement to basic packet switching.

Take the example of traditional digital telephony. The analog voice signal is sampled at a rate of 8 kHz. Each sample is digitized using an 8-bit log scale, resulting in a 64-kbit per second data stream. This signal can be sent over the Internet as a succession of packets. Popular programs such as "vat" will packetize the data stream, typically packing 160 samples that represent 20 milliseconds of voice, into one Internet packet. They will send 50 packets per second through the Internet. If the transmission is reasonably steady, this receiver will be able to unpack the voice samples and to play back an undistorted voice signal. But the quality drops when the network is congested. Some packets will experience long queues. This will result in a very long play-out delay, reducing the interactivity of the communication. Other packets will be lost, which will result in crackles.

Delays and crackles result from the traditional scheduling policies of packet switches. Whoever comes first is served first, much in the same ways as clients in a supermarket or cars on a highway. Reservation procedures aim at creating a special lane for some well-identified packets. They are based on theoretical studies that showed how specific scheduling policies can be implemented in packet switches to guarantee a steady flow of packets. The IETF has been working since 1993 on a resource reservation protocol called RSVP. We will detail how the IPv6 labeling of flows can be used in conjunction with this protocol. We will also present how some researchers envisage using hop by hop options for explicating the requirements of flows, as well as the potential relation between reservation procedures and ATM networks.

6.2.1 Special Services

Traditional packet switches do not try to mess with packet queuing. When a packet is received, it is passed to the routing module, which examines its destination address and determines the outcoming line. If this line is available, the packet is transmitted immediately. Otherwise, the packet is queued for later transmission. This policy is called *first come, first served*. There is one single queue in front of each outgoing line.

One Queue per Outgoing Line

This traditional behavior is not mandatory, however. Instead of having exactly one queue per outgoing interface, switches may decide to classify packets. They may, for example, give priority to the queue of real-time packets over that of data packets. But this would not be enough. If we want real guarantees, we must be sure that a queue that sends 50 packets per second will be visited 50 times per second. To use the queuing theory's vocabulary, we must be sure that the *service rate* will be equal to or higher than the *arrival rate* of a given queue. One way to achieve this is to have one queue per real-time communication and also one default queue for all data packets.

In our example, we picture four real-time flows. The flow label can be used, in conjunction with the source address, to assert which packets belong to what flows. By default, packets that are not recognized as part of one real-time flow will be part of the default data queue. A reservation procedure will be used to declare the real-time flows, and to inform the routers of their requirements. Each real-time flow will be serviced at a rate compatible with its requirements. It

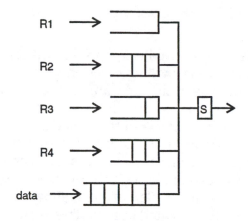

— Four Real-Time Flows and Data Queue —

will never suffer from unpredictable queuing delays, and it will also not experience congestion. The data queue, on the other hand, will only be serviced on a best effort basis. As a consequence of reserving transmission resources for the real-time flows, it will only receive whatever capacity is left. It will experience longer delays and more frequent congestions.

6.2.2 Using RSVP and Flows

In the Internet, the reservation protocol of choice is called RSVP. The key assumption of RSVP is that resource reservation will mostly be needed for multicast applications, such as high-speed video transmission. These applications have some peculiar characteristics, like a large number of receivers that may be experiencing very different transmission conditions and that may also belong to different domains. As a consequence, RSVP is a *receiver-driven* protocol. It is up to the receivers to select which source they want to receive, and how much bandwidth they are ready to reserve and, in commercial networks, pay for. They do so by sending RSVP messages to the network.

Sources enable reservation by regularly sending PATH messages, alongside the regular data messages. Through these PATH messages, the Internet routers acquire knowledge of ongoing communications. The RSVP messages will be propagated on the reverse path marked by the PATH messages so as to make sure that resources are reserved on the exact link that is used to propagate the data.

A typical RSVP message will explain the address of the source, or sources, that the receiver wants to listen to, the address of the multicast group onto which the data are sent, and some quality of service parameters (e.g., the data rate to be reserved). It will also contain a *filter* that specifies the *profile* of the data that the receiver wants to select. Suppose, for example, that a file transfer is going on between A and B at the same time as an audio conversation. One wishes to reserve 64 kbps of bandwidth for the audio, but one certainly does not want to see the file transfer compete for that reserved bandwidth and destroy the sound quality. This is exactly what filters are for.

Specifying the filters in IPv4 requires a layer violation. The file transfer uses TCP and the audio uses UDP. But filtering on the protocol type alone is not sufficient, since there may well be several simultaneous TCP and UDP applications. One must also specify the UDP and TCP ports.

Layer violations are indeed not capital sins. Many networkers will be very satisfied to just specify the UDP ports in complement to the source and destination addresses. But with IPv6, the port numbers may end up being buried deep inside the packets, behind a long daisy chain of extension headers. This would make the filtering code very inefficient. Worse still, port numbers will not be visible at all if the packets are encrypted. This is where IPv6 flow labels can be used. Instead of specifying port numbers, the receiver can mention in their filters the label of the particular flows that they want to privilege. This information will be present up front in the packet and easy to access, making the classifying process very efficient and easy to implement.

6.2.3 Using Hop-by-Hop Options

We must mention that RSVP is not the only reservation procedure that could be implemented with IPv6. Some researchers believe that they can define the quality of service requirements of a given flow in a hop by hop option. This option would be transmitted in some packets. The routers would remember the associated parameters and associate them with the flow.

6.3 Modern Handling of Multimedia

Back in 1992, audio and video were considered hard real-time applications for which the reservation of resources was absolutely necessary, unless you were ready for massively overprovisioning the network. MBONE was still in infancy. In fact, the first video transmissions over the Internet took place approximately when the first versions of SIP were drafted. Since then, we have made a lot of progress in handling multimedia over the Internet. We have understood that these applications can in fact adapt to a wide range of networking conditions. We found out that *fair queuing* may well be a more effective way of sharing network resources than reservations, specially when combined with procedures such as *class-based queuing*. We started to implement *hierarchical-encoding*, which enables even more effective adaptations of multimedia applications to networking conditions.

6.3.1 Adaptive Applications

In 1988, Van Jacobson revised the classic implementation of the TCP protocol. He used classic results of the control theory to design the slow start algorithm. From now on, the TCP connection will start up at a minimal speed and increase gradually in order not to destabilize the network. The TCP programs will include a feedback loop that will automatically slow down the application if the network becomes congested. The results have been spectacular, but the advent of uncontrolled or open-loop multimedia application is threatening to bring the network back to its chaotic pre-1988 state.

Multimedia application should not have to be open loop. When we deployed our first implementation of the Inria Videoconferencing System, IVS, in 1992, we quickly realized that there was no such thing as a fixed rate requirement for video. Our user interface featured a sliding ruler that allowed the user to select a data rate between 16 and 256 kbps. This data rate translated internally in a compression ratio, trading video quality and network usage. By 1994, we had included in our program a feedback control algorithm. The program continuously collects transmission reports from all the recipients, using a scalable sensing strategy designed jointly with our partners at University College London. If congestion is detected, the transmission ratio is immediately decreased. It is slowly increased when everything looks fine. By adopting the same behavior as Van Jacobson's TCP, we minimized the impact of video transmission on classic usage of the Internet.

Since 1994, we have pursued our researches. Laboratory experiments show that video is by no means an exception. Other real-time applications, in fact most of them, can be rendered *network conscious* by incorporating feedback control algorithms. A good example is that of *distributed simulations*: the position and speed of objects are broadcast to all players at regular intervals so that each can obtain a consistent view of the playing field. By resorting to dead reckoning, one may space the transmissions to fit the network capabilities; this is similar to adapting the frame rate of a video transmission. One may also play with the size of the messages, giving more or less information about the objects' shapes, colors, or capabilities; this is similar to adapting the video's definition. In fact, the most difficult case appears to be that of voice transmission. The available transmission algorithms have been designed for circuit-switched telephony; they are ill fitted for packet network. Research, however, is progressing. High-quality adaptive voice transmission should be available before 1996.

6.3.2 Enforcing Fairness

Simulation studies show that, if all stations in a test Internet implement Van Jacobson's slow start algorithm, the network is well utilized and all users get an approximately equal share of the resource. In a sense, this is optimal and fair. The same simulations will, however, show that slight differences between the station's parameters may result in important differences between the share of the network that they get. For example, if some stations are nearer than the others to a network's bottleneck, they will react faster to situations of congestion, starting to transmit sooner when the congestion ceases. Similarly, if one tweaks a station's parameter and makes it more aggressive than its peers, that station ends up transmitting faster.

This situation was acceptable when the Internet was populated by research scientists. They had a strong sense of belonging to a privileged community. Social pressure was sufficient to guarantee that everybody would play by the rules, that everybody's TCP would implement a correct version of the congestion avoidance algorithm. But the social pressure gets diluted as the Internet reaches the masses. Networks should not trust users to behave fairly; they should enforce fairness, for example by some form of fair queuing.

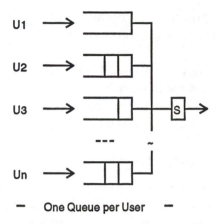

— One Queue per User —

The basic idea of *fair queuing* is that packets are classified within queues and that each queue gets the same amount of resources. The assignment of packets to queues is very similar to the classification of packets in flows when reservations are used. Different implementations may use different classes. Some will set one class per source address; others will have one class per destination address or one class per TCP connection. But there is no explicit reservation. The policy merely enforces that each user gets a fair share, even if some of them are trying to play foul with the rules.

6.3.3 Class-based Queuing

Having a fair share for each user is only one part of the picture. Fairness, like beauty, is often in the eyes of the beholder. Is it fair to give the same service to the virtual tourist in a web museum and to the surgeon who is advising on an open-heart operation? In practice, users are not all equal. The full picture is one of hierarchical classes.

At the broadest level, we find classes assigned to whole organizations. For example, my organization, INRIA, could well specify in its contract with our network provider, Renater, that under situations of congestion we will always get at least 8% of the available capacity. A hospital will have a similar arrangement with its local provider, guaranteeing that sufficient resources will always be made available when needed for tele-surgeons. Other large customers may have similar arrangements. This means that when a packet arrives it is first assigned to one of these superclasses. Within each class we will have a secondary classification, for example, an implementation of fair queuing among the variable sources or a sharing of resources between reserved flows and plain data traffic.

In short, we may expect that the traffic will be policed, that a given user, a given flow, will only be capable of transmitting a well-defined quantity of packets per unit of time. If one tries to send more than the available, capacity some packets will be dropped.

6.3.4 Hierarchical Coding

Senders should always try to get the best quality of service out of the available capacity. Algorithms like TCP's slow start do exactly that for normal data transfer. They keep the pipe almost constantly full, while avoiding too frequent losses that would jeopardize the efficiency of TCP. Real-time applications could mimic the behavior of TCP. They would try to assess the available capacity and then tune the sampling rates and the compression ratios so as to remain within that capacity. But there are at least two cases when this adaptation cannot be performed efficiently:

- It takes some time for an application to discover the available capacity. If the network state is changing faster than this adaptation period, we will observe cycles, transient congestions, and packet losses.
- The paths leading to the various members of large multicast groups may all have different capacities. The absence of loss can only be guaranteed if one adapts to the lowest of these capacities, leading in practice to the worst possible service.

The favorite solution in our little circle of researchers is called *hierarchical coding*. Suppose that we want to transmit a sound signal. The sound is captured with a high-fidelity microphone and sampled at 44 kHz with 16 bits of precision. We can organize the transmission as a hierarchy of packets:

- A basic packet, containing a subsampling of the signal at 5.5 kHz,
- A complementary packet containing the difference between the 5.5- and an 11-kHz sampling
- Two more packets containing the difference between the 11- and 22- kHz samplings
- Four packets containing the differences between 22 kHz and the full-precision 44-kHz sampling

Each packet will have a different priority code so that if the link is congested the 44-kHz packets are dropped first, then the 22-kHz packets, and then the 11-kHz packets. This way, we make sure that

■ Even if the network changes status very fast, the user's share will always be filled with useful data.

■ Even if the members of a multicast group have very different capacities, they will all get the best quality of service compatible with their local paths.

In short, hierarchical coding enables the applications to prioritize their data so that the most significant bits get dropped last. Hierarchical coding is supported by the drop priority label, which is encoded as a 4-bit integer in the first octet of the IPv6 header:

| Version | Priority | | Flow Label | |

The IPv6 specification reserves the priority values 0 to 7 to the congestion-controlled traffic, whose transmission control procedure includes congestion control loops identical or similar to Van Jacobson's slow start. This traffic is classified according to its relative priority, from 1 for the least urgent data to 7 for the internet control traffic.

```
0  ―  uncharacterized traffic
1  ―  "filler" traffic (e.g., netnews)
2  ―  unattended data  transfer (e.g., email)
3  ―  (reserved)
4  ―  attended bulk transfer (e.g., FTP, NFS)
5  ―  (reserved)
6  ―  interactive traffic (e.g., telnet, X)
7  ―  internet control traffic (e.g., routing protocols, SNMP)
```

―   Priority Classes for Congestion-controlled Traffic   ―

The codes 8 to 15 are reserved for real-time traffic, or rather noncongestion-controlled traffic. The highest value, 15, is reserved for the packets that contain the most significant part of the information, while the value 8 is reserved for the least important part. In our example, the 5.5-kHz packets could be tagged with priority 15. Decreasing priorities would then be used for 11, 22, and 44 kHz. When several media are used in parallel, the priorities should be assigned according to their relative importance. For example, all our trials show that video communication is a luxury that can only be afforded if a good quality audio is already available. If we want to transmit simultaneously audio and video, we will probably play with the priority, maybe assigning to slow scan video a priority intermediate between 11- and 22-kHz audio, then a priority intermediate between 22- and 44-kHz audio for low-definition video. Finally, the code 8 will be used for high-fidelity video.

Priorities are relative. They are used to rank the packets of one single source, not to compare those of multiple sources. They can only be used in complement to queuing policies such as fair queuing or class-based queuing. Once the router has determined that some packets of a given source must be dropped, it should look at the priority field and start with those that have the lowest priority value.

One should also note that there is no implied ordering between the controlled and the real-time traffic. Obviously, high-definition video packets should not be given priority over SNMP traffic, even if one is tagged 8 and the other 7!

6.4 Points of Controversy

We have to support real-time applications in the Internet. In fact, some of them are already here. In the last months, I have been able to use the Internet and

- Take part from France in a conference in London, interactively
- Click on a web icon and see a videoclip, but see it instantly, without having to first copy umpteen megabytes of MPEG data on my hard disk
- Click on a colleague personal web page and be immediately connected to him through video and audio

These applications are already coming out of the research laboratories and more are coming, for example distributed virtual reality. This is certainly the Internet's next frontier. We could then expect a wide consensus on the inclusion of real-time support in IPv6. We would be disappointed. Controversy rages. I tried to pick here three topics that have received a lot of attention: the usefulness of flow labels, the need to support reservations, and the relation between IPv6 and ATM.

6.4.1 Will Flow Labels Be Used?

Flow labels were designed as a tool for expediting several routing functions. The packets that originate from the same source and bear the same flow label share several characteristics:

- They are all bound to the same destination and should all be fowarded to the same next hop,
- They all belong to the same reservation group or queuing class.
- They all have the same hop by hop options and routing header, if option or routing headers are present.

One could very well imagine that routers maintain a table of the currently active flows, associating the flow label with the next hop, the queuing class, and possibly an indication of special actions, such as hop by hop options or routing header updates. Routers would create a line in the cache whenever they see a new flow label, discarding the least recently used entry. In fact, the choice of assigning random numbers to flows is meant to facilitate their use as access key in a table of flows.

Many routers do already maintain similar caches, associating currently active destinations and next hops. The caches are not searched linearly for each packet. Routers compute a hash code of the destination address and use it as the access key. The idea of assigning pseudorandom numbers to the flow labels is precisely grounded in this practice. The hashing algorithms derive a pseudo-random number that represents the destination address. The label is a precomputed random number that also represents the destination. The precomputation may save three or four computer instructions inside one of the most critical parts of the router's software.

But, then, one should take a second look. Relying on flow labels for software optimization is problematic because it is only a partial solution and also because the number of flows is likely to be larger than the number of sources or destinations.

IPv6 stations are not required to assign all packets to flows. They always have the option to use a null flow label. One may expect that at least during the transition period, they will simply use this option. The router that relies on the presence of labels to expedite packet processing will end up using the unlabeled packet exception for a very significant portion of its traffic, with the associated performance hit.

There are more flows than sources. In practice, we observe that the number of network partners of any station tends to grow with the size of the network, albeit very slowly. Thus the number of source-destination pairs grows faster than the size of the network. Because there can be more than one flow per source-destination pair, we can safely assume that the number of currently active flows will be significantly larger than either the number of active sources or the number of active destinations. This increased number may translate in less cache hits for the same amount of memory, maybe offsetting the few instructions gained by not hashing the destination address.

In fact, we are here entirely in a domain of vaporware and hypothesis. The only conclusion that we can hold for certain is that flow labels are a useful tool for designating packets that belong to reservation groups.

6.4.2 To Reserve or Not?

Most network engineers learned in school that you need a real-time network to support a real-time service. We saw in the previous sections of this chapter that this is not quite true: we can build intelligent applications that adapt to networking conditions by means of play-out buffers and either feedback control and adaptive coding, or priority droppings and hierarchical coding. But the fact remains that if one wants to predict an application's quality of service one must obtain guarantees of service from the network. At this point of reasoning, we can draw two conclusions:

- Some believe that we must be able to provide guarantees of service in the future Internet, which implies that we must provide a reservation service.
- Others believe that this deployment is unneeded and that we should simply provide more capacity, control resource assignment through some variation of fair queuing, and develop adaptive applications.

In fact, there is little doubt that we should develop adaptive applications in any case. Reservation procedures may have the effect that one communication will receive a better share of the existing communication resource, but they will not increase that resource. If a station is connected through a noisy radio channel, reservation procedures will not suddenly transform that radio channel into a high-capacity optical fiber. The Internet is a network of networks that uses many different technologies. Transmission conditions will always be variable. We need applications that do their best out of the available bandwidth.

Reservation procedures are mostly a way to handle scarcity. Suppose that we use fair queuing. Users would only need to reserve more resources if their share was not sufficient for their application. But by allocating more bandwidth to some users, one deprives others of their legitimate resources. If all of them try to reserve bandwidth, some reservations will have to be refused, and some network users will be very dissatisfied. Soon, managers will realize that they should increase the network's capacity or see their users leave for better providers. If they had increased the capacity in the first place, they would have saved on reservation management and accounting procedure.

Some adaptive applications are already being marketed. They have the property that they do not need any reservation, appear just like regular Internet application, yet are not flow controlled. Because they do not require anything special in the middle of the network, they can be easily deployed. Network managers will soon realize that they need to implement explicit resource allocation policies. They are very likely to just turn on the fair queuing software that is already present in many routers, giving a premium to the adaptive applications.

The debate is not over. In fact, we may well end up with a limited deployment of reservation procedures for special usages in controlled environments, while the bulk of the real-time exchanges over the Internet will just use adaptive applications that take advantage of IPv6 support for drop priorities.

6.4.3 What about ATM?

To quote Steve Deering, the three most important requirements of real-time multimedia communications are bandwidth, bandwidth, and bandwidth. If we believe the current advertisement campaign of the traditional telecommunication companies, more bandwidth requires that we switch to their last creation, asynchronous transfer mode or ATM. Some go as far as saying that the Internet will soon be replaced by ATM networks. Indeed, these networks are not quite developed yet, even if their imminent arrival has been announced for several years. But according to their promoters they will be ready really soon now, and we will have to adopt or die.

Saying that many Internet developers are somewhat irritated by this hype would be a serious understatement. The ATM technology features about everything that the telecommunication industry likes and thus could not be more antagonistic to our culture. We know by experience that circuit switching does not fit the needs of computer communication, yet the ATM network is based on virtual circuits, not datagrams. We know by experience that we can only scale networks to a large size if they are as simple as possible, yet ATM networks try to provide a full range of quality of services at the expense of extreme management complexity. We know by experience that the unit of transmission, the datagram, should be the unit of control that is acknowledged and repeated by transport protocol, yet the ATM designers picked a very small cell size. In conditions of congestion, when a 48-octet cell is lost, a frame of 20 to 100 cells must be repeated, with a dramatic impact on performance. It is thus hardly a surprise if our favorite version of the ATM acronym is "Another Terrible Mistake."

Looking at ATM with cold eyes does not imply that we should entirely ignore it. In fact, it is amazing to observe that the first demonstrations of the ATM network capabilities were done by running the Internet Protocol on top of ATM. Integrating IP over ATM is actually very easy. It suffices to define a framing structure for carrying the IP packets as a set of ATM cells. From a networking point of view, there is very little difference between ATM virtual circuits and X.25 virtual circuits, which we have been using for a long time. As long as ATM networks do not provide dynamic switching, ATM permanent virtual circuits will be used as links within an IP network, just like the existing T1 or T3 channels. When dynamic switching becomes available, circuits could be established on demand. This is where the debate starts on how much ATM support IPv6 should include.

We heard the same debate with X.25 and then with ISDN. Traditional telecommunication providers would love to sell relatively narrow circuits at retail price, rather than transmission capacity in bulk. To do so, they have always pressed for a linkage between end usage and capacity allocation. For example, they suggested that an X.25 or ISDN circuit be set up when one user starts a connection with a remote computer. They suggest now that an ATM virtual circuit be set up for each TCP connection or for each multimedia association. The reasoning is that quality of service guarantees can only be provided if the network knows exactly the applications' requirements.

The side effect is that the customer's bill inflates with each connection request.

All our experience with the Internet technology tells us that this traditional approach is entirely wrong. Packet switching allows us to multiplex several applications on the same channel on the same infrastructure. This infrastructure has a fixed cost that can be predicted in yearly budgets. ATM's quality of service provisions may have been an adequate answer to the multimedia requirements that were perceived 15 years ago, when ATM was first designed, when adaptive multimedia applications were not yet developed. Today's requirement is much simpler. We need a lot of bandwidth at the lowest possible price. This certainly means buying in bulk, not at retail prices. Besides, there is every reason to believe that ATM will not be the sole technology in future networks.

- For low-end stations, simple Ethernet attachments are much simpler and much more cost effective than ATM interfaces.
- For the middle range, Ethernet switches and the fast 100-Mbps Ethernet networks are a very effective competition to ATM switches.
- At the high end, technologies like HIPPI, Fiber-Channel, or Myrinet already provide throughputs of 650 Mbps.
- In wide areas, IPv6 could well run directly on top of Sonet connections, removing the ATM overhead.
- In mobile networks, the very idea of maintaining virtual circuits looks absurd.

In short, the network of the future will incorporate some ATM circuits, but it would be stupid to entirely rely on the ATM technology. There will thus be only limited support for ATM within IPv6.

- Even if flow labels are present, flows are not virtual circuits. There is no flow setup procedure, and there are not necessarily any quality of service parameters associated with flows. By default, flow-labeled packets will just be routed like ordinary datagrams.
- Routers may, however, decide to buy bandwidth on demand in situations of congestion or in order to serve the requirements that receivers expressed through the reservation protocol, RSVP.

As for many other points of controversy, the relation between IPv6 and ATM will ultimately be solved by market forces.

6.5 Further Reading

The structure of flow labels and priority codes is described in the main IPv6 specification. Craig Partridge wrote a memorandum on the use of flows in IPv6 that should soon be published as an RFC.

The RSVP protocol was described by Lixia Zhang, Steve Deering, Deborah Estrin, Scott Shenker, and David Zappala in an article, "RSVP: A New Resource ReSerVation Protocol," published in *IEEE Network* in September 1993. The final version of the specifications should soon be published as an RFC.

The case for fair queuing is well expressed in a communication by Scott Shenker to the 1994 Sigcomm conference, "Making Greed Work in Networks: A Game Theoretic Analysis of Switch Service Disciplines." An analysis of fair queuing can be found in an article published by A. Demers, S. Keshav, and S. Shenker, "Analysis and Simulation of a Fair Queueing Algorithm," in the first issue of the *Journal of Internetworking: Research and Experience*, in 1990.

Van Jacobson described the slow start and congestion avoidance algorithm in a communication to the 1988 Sigcomm conference, "Congestion Avoidance and Control." He coauthored with Sally Floyd an article in the August 1993 issue of the *IEEE/ACM Transactions on Networking*, "Random Early Detection Gateway for Congestion Avoidance," describing the random early drop policy, a possible alternative to the implementation of fair queuing.

On the relation between IP and ATM, I can recommend the communication by Allyn Romanow and Sally Floyd to the 1994 Sigcomm Symposium, "Dynamics of TCP Traffic over ATM networks."

Transitioning the Internet

Pv6, in theory, is just a new version of IP, a new release of the IP software. Someday, your computer will receive an upgrade that makes it IPv6 capable. Once all the computers in the Internet have received this new version and turned it on, we will have achieved the transition to IPv6, and the Internet will be ready to link to millions of billions of stations. But we have first to walk the path of transition.

7.1 Dual-Stack Strategy

After much deliberation, which we will describe in the section on controversies, the Internet community decided that the transition from IPv4 to IPv6 will follow a dual-stack strategy. An IPv6 Internet will be deployed in parallel to the existing IPv4 Internet, possibly by borrowing some of its infrastructure. At the beginning of the transition period, all IPv6-capable hosts will also be IPv4 capable so as to retain connectivity with the existing Internet. The choice to use either stack will be based on information provided by the name service.

7.1.1 Supporting Two IP Layers

Although IPv6 and IPv4 protocols are different in details, they are very similar in principle. This similarity ensures that only minor developments are required to transform an IPv4 station into a dual-stack, IPv6-capable host. The list of required upgrades includes:

- The IPv6 code, essentially the basic IPv6, ICMP, and neighbor discovery code
- The handling of IPv6 within the transport protocols TCP and UDP
- Modifications to the "sockets" or "winsock" libraries to support IPv6 addresses and the IPv6 interface extensions
- The interface with the name service

Neither of these modifications is very large. One can probably program them all within a few kilobytes of code.

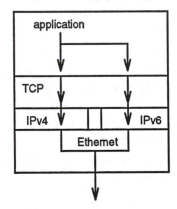

Typical Dual-Stack Configuration

The worst part of supporting two stacks in parallel is probably the need to manage two different sets of addresses. But the automatic neighbor discovery procedures of IPv6 should make this task almost invisible to the manager, especially if we compare it to the cost of configuring IPv4 stations today.

Upgrading a router to support IPv6 is indeed slightly more complex. The router must be equipped with the IPv6 packet forwarding code, the IPv6 routing protocols, and the IPv6 management protocols, not to forget the IPv6 transition mechanisms. For a router, there is very little overlap between the IPv6 and IPv4 codes. In fact, many routers are already programmed to support several other protocols than IP, for example Novell's IPX, Apple's Appletalk, or IBM's System Network Architecture. IPv6 will just be one more element in this list.

7.1.2 Name Servers and Decisions

Applications are not supposed to directly handle addresses such as 123.45.67.89 or 1234:4567:89AB:CDEF:FEDC:BA98:7654:4321. This would not be user friendly, because typing many numbers is cumbersome and error prone. It would also be dangerous in terms of management, because new automatic configuration procedures will make renumbering very easy. The address that the user remembered, or copied in a file, may well have changed and been given to another host. Applications should definitely handle names, not addresses.

The dual-stack strategy relies heavily on the domain name service. A dual-stack host will have several address records in the DNS, one A record per IPv4 address and one AAAA record per IPv6 address. The current *gethostbyname* interface, which enables applications to get the IPv4 address corresponding to a domain name, will be replaced by a new interface, *hostname2addr*. Gethostbyname is called with only one argument, the target's name. Hostname2addr will have two arguments, the target's name and the address family, either AF_INET for IPv4 addresses or AF_INET6 for IPv6 addresses.

If the argument is AF_INET, the procedure returns one address per A record present in the target's DNS entry. If the argument is AF_INET6, the procedure will first query the DNS for the target's AAAA records. If any are found, they will be returned. Otherwise, the procedure will query the DNS again, this time asking for the target IPv4 addresses. It will return these addresses as IPv4-mapped IPv6 addresses.

Dual-stack hosts will use the new resolution procedure. They will then pick the best address out of the returned list and use that address in the TCP connection request or as a destination address for the UDP datagrams. The dual-stack transport protocols will decide either to use IPv6 if the address is a plain IPv6 address or simply to use IPv4 if the address is a mapped IPv4 address.

As the deployment progresses, an increasing proportion of the Internet hosts will receive IPv6 addresses and document them in the DNS. The transition will take place naturally, as more and more connections use IPv6. There will not be any flag day, but rather a flowing tide that will eventually take over the whole Internet.

7.1.3 Critical Points of Transition

The dual-stack transition assumes that the name service will be immediately updated to support the AAAA records. This is a very simple modification. It took me only a few days of work to integrate the support for SIP in the *bind* software in January 1993, and I did not need to write more than 50 lines of code. One may expect that supporting IPv6 will not be any more complex. Clients and servers will indeed have to deploy the new software version, but even that should not be problematic. The DNS protocols are transparent to the content of records. Only those servers and interfaces that need to provide or access IPv6 addresses have to be actually upgraded. Deploying these servers will be part of the deployment of IPv6 within organizations' networks.

But we must also make sure that the new version is operational, that a fully connected IPv6 Internet is present from the start. Otherwise, the upgraded applications will find addresses in the DNS, will try to set up TCP connections toward these addresses, and will see the connections fail. This connectivity will be initially provided by an overlay structure over the Internet built out of tunnels connecting islands. We have already some experience in this deployment with the experimental multicast backbone, the MBone. By analogy, the initial experimental IPv6 structure will probably be called the 6-Bone.

This structure should not only be present and operational. It should also have good performance, at the very least similar to that of the regular Internet connections. If the 6-Bone is too slow, users will quickly discover that IPv6-capable hosts have lesser performance than plain IPv4 hosts. Very soon, they would disable the IPv6 capacity!

7.2 Building the 6-Bone

It is very easy to deploy IPv6 on a single local network. We just need to install IPv6-capable software in the local computers and to connect one IPv6-capable router. Dynamic address configuration and neighbor discovery will operate immediately. If the router is connected to several IPv6-capable local networks, we will be able to install IPv6 connectivity within a routing domain. But we will only have built an IPv6 island in an ocean of IPv4 networks. IPv6 datagrams can be exchanged within the domain, the island, but they will not cross over to other islands without bridges, or rather tunnels

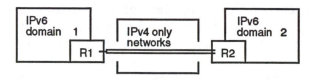

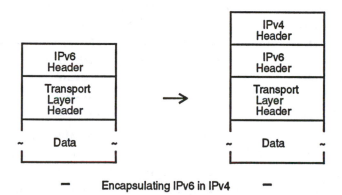

— Connecting Two Islands through a Tunnel —

IPv6 routers that are separated from others by a set of IPv4 only networks can build up a virtual link by configuring a tunnel, bringing up connectivity between the two networks. IPv6 packets traveling from one domain to another will be encapsulated within an IPv4 packet traveling between the two routers.

— Encapsulating IPv6 in IPv4 —

The tunnels will be characterized by the two end-point IPv4 addresses, as well as some ancillary control parameters such as the tunnel's MTU and time to live, which should be chosen with care. The IPv4 protocol identifier will be set to 41, the assigned payload type number for IPv6.

The tunneling strategy was followed rather successfully in the multicast backbone. The deployment of the MBone started in the spring of 1992, when Steve Casner organized the first multicasting of the sound track of an IETF conference. Within a few years, the MBone grew to link tens of thousands of stations. But we also learned from this experience that tunnels should be configured with care, that they may lead to very strange routing decisions. Finally, we will also have to consider the undoing of these tunnels.

7.2.1 Choosing the MTU

One control parameter of any tunnel is the maximum size of the packets that can be forwarded through it. In principle, as IPv4 can support fragmentation and reassembly, the only limit is the maximum size of an IPv4 packet, 65,536 octets, minus 20 octets for the IPv4 header itself. However, the same reasons that led to removing the fragmentation procedure from IPv6 teach us that we should be more careful. If we allow large packets to be sent over the tunnel, the router at the other end will receive a lot of small fragments. It will have to spend a lot of time and memory in the reassembly procedures. If fragments are lost, the remaining fragments will eat up buffer space until their TTL times out. The whole IPv6 packet will be lost and will have to be retransmitted. In short, fragmentation is just as harmful within tunnels as between hosts.

To reduce fragmentation to a minimum, the routers at both ends should track the tunnel's MTU. They can, in fact, very easily perform their own version of the generic IPv4 MTU discovery procedure. They will initiate the tunnel's MTU to the MTU of their local interface. If ICMP messages come back to indicate that the packet was too big, they will switch to a lower MTU. Occasionally, they may send a test message to detect a possible increase in the MTU.

As long as the tunnel's MTU remains larger than the IPv6 minimum supported packet size of 576 octets, the IPv4 fragmentation will be turned off in the IPv4 header. If an IPv6 packet larger than the tunnel's MTU is presented to the interface, it will be discarded and an IPv6 *packet too big* ICMP message will be sent back to the user. But the IPv4 minimum packet size is only 48 octets, not 576. Tunnel's MTU may occasionally be lower than 576 octets, which will force IPv6 routers into a controlled use of IPv4 segmentation:

> 1. *If the IPv4 tunnel MTU is lower than 576 octets, IPv6 packets larger than 576 octets will be discarded, and a packet too big message will be sent back to the IPv6 sender. This packet will indicate a maximum IPv6 MTU of 576 octets.*

> 2. *If the IPv6 packet is not larger than the tunnel MTU, IPv4 fragmentation will not be used.*

> 3. *If the IPv6 packet is larger than the tunnel MTU but not larger than 576, IPv4 fragmentation will be allowed.*

Using MTU discovery will normally ensure that IPv6 users get the best performance from IPv4 tunnels.

7.2.2 Tunnels and Routing Protocols

Once tunnels are configured, they will be treated just as any other kind of link in the global IPv6 infrastructure. If the tunnel is used to link two separate routing domains, it will be used for exchanging routes, using IDRP. If the tunnel falls entirely within a routing domain, it will be considered as a plain serial link by interior routing protocols such as RIP or OSPF.

But tunnels are not plain serial links. Consider the case of RIP, whose metric is the number of hops. By default, the tunnel's cost will be set to 1, just like a direct link between two routers, although the tunneled packets are in fact relayed several times by IPv4 layers. This may result in strange choices, like preference for routing through a long tunnel instead of relaying through a small number of direct IPv6 connections.

Our experience with the MBone teaches us that tunnels' metrics should be chosen with great care in order to avoid these distortions. One solution would be to manually assign a tunnel metric, which could be derived from an expected throughput for OSPF or an expected number of relays for RIP. This would guarantee that the nominal routes will follow a reasonable path. But one should also take into account the inherent variability of these metrics. Consider the case of a tunnel between the domains A and B. In a nominal configuration, it is relayed through two intermediate domains, T and U. But if the direct link between X and Y is broken, the tunneled packets will take a detour through V and W, a path that is three times longer and probably also much more congested.

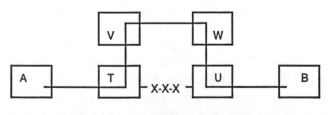

Tunnels May Sometimes Be Longer Than Expected

In the case of the MBone, the choice was either to suffer until the routes are reestablished or to manually update the tunnel's metric if the critical outage was expected to last so that another tunnel will be preferred. This is one of the most painful parts of operating an overlay network. Within a single routing domain, the manager's task could be made easier if the choice of the tunnel's metric was somehow automated, if the IPv6 routing process could derive the tunnel's metric from the IPv4 routing tables. But this is still vaporware.

7.2.3 Time to Live in a Tunnel

Because IPv4 routing is dynamic, the time spent by packets in a tunnel will vary. Packets should be sent through a tunnel with a sufficient IPv4 TTL to guarantee that they will not time out en route. The current specification of transition mechanisms is rather elliptic on this point. It merely says that the TTL is chosen in an implementation-dependent manner, that the default value should be that suggested in the current assigned numbers RFC, or 64 as per RFC 1700.

One could in fact set up this TTL dynamically, in much the same way as the *traceroute* program. Monitoring the tunnel's TTL can be useful if one wants to quickly discover changes in the IPv4 routing and update the tunnel's metric accordingly.

Whatever the IPv4 TTL value, a tunnel will always be considered a single hop for the IPv6 packet, just like a simple serial link. The hop count will be decremented by exactly one unit when the packet is relayed.

7.2.4 Controlling the Tunnel's Share

One of the drawbacks of layered routing is that it messes up resource control. The tunneled packets will compete for transmission resources with plain IPv4 packets. The matter could be even worse if the IPv4 routers use fair queuing, because the tunnel will just get a single user's share of the resource, although it represents in fact a whole set of IPv6 users.

A similar problem was encountered in the MBone, although for a different reason. The MBone multicast packets carried real-time applications that were not congestion controlled. In situations of congestion, these applications would not back off, causing regular TCP-controlled applications to use ever decreasing windows. The MBone problem was solved by enforcing a nominal bandwidth for the critical MBone tunnels. The multicast routing process will pace the transmission of multicast packets accordingly.

A similar solution could be used for IPv6 tunnels. It has several advantages:

- Managers can control the share of the network that will be allocated to IPv6.

- The IPv6 resource controls, such as resource reservation, fair queuing, or drop priorities, can be enforced before sending packets in a tunnel.

- The tunnel bandwidth can be used to assign a realistic metric to the tunnel.

There are also some potential disadvantages. By definition, enforcing a rate limit for the IPv6 tunnel means that IPv6 packets will not be able to take advantage of resources unused by plain IPv4 packets. Also, if the corresponding bandwidth is not effectively reserved at the IPv4 level, the IPv6-level policing will not guarantee that high-priority packets are not discarded somewhere in the middle of the tunnel.

This is clearly a point where further studies could help. One might imagine a dynamic tunnel management protocol monitoring the bandwidth available to the tunnel in real time and policing the IPv6 flow accordingly. But this is a very tricky control problem, because there are very complex interactions between the control variable, the rate at which packets are sent in the tunnel, and the observed tunnel capacity. Setting a predefined bandwidth and enforcing it at the IPv4 level is much simpler and probably much more stable. A fast deployment of native IPv6 capabilities would be even better, because we would get rid of tunnels!

7.2.5 Digging Tunnels and Closing Them

We cannot ignore basic rules of networking. Multiples layers of routing and queuing are just as harmful as multiple layers of fragmentation. We can avoid fragmentation by a judicious choice of the tunnels' MTU. We should avoid layered routing as much as possible by only configuring a minimal number of tunnels. We should also try to make our tunnels short so as to minimize their variance. The rule is in fact very simple. Whenever it is available, direct IPv6 routing should be preferred to tunnels.

Yakov Rekhter observed, during the discussion of the transition process, that we could probably use the information on adjacent domains provided by BGP to design the setup of routers. One can extract from BGP's autonomous system paths the list of neighboring autonomous systems. Going from there to the list of neighboring external routers, either directly connected or a few hops away is a simple matter. One could then poll these routers to check their IPv6 capability. One could even envisage setting up tunnels automatically, although the MBone experience tells us that managers will like to keep some control.

The BGP tables are in fact only one source of information. We may expect the development of routing aides, IPv6 versions of traceroute, and special programs that test the 6-Bone's configuration.

7.3 Connecting End Stations

In the previous section, we reviewed the use of tunnels by routers as a way to establish the initial IPv6 connectivity. But tunnels may also be used by hosts, either in a configured way or in an automatic fashion.

Let's examine the case of an isolated IPv6 host. It has repeated router solicitations on its various network interfaces, but no router has responded. In the absence of a router, it can only speak IPv6 to its immediate neighbors, other IPv6 hosts connected to the same interfaces. In the initial phase of transition, this should not be a real problem. All IPv6 hosts will also be IPv4 capable, all IPv6 servers will also be reachable through IPv4 and the IPv4-only host will not be deprived of any service. But, as the transition progresses, this situation will change. Because we do not want to introduce another flag day, it is important to make sure that even isolated IPv6 hosts can get access to the IPv6 Internet.

IPv6 hosts will use the IPv4 network as a virtual interface that enables them to reach other hosts or routers through tunnels. They can configure this interface with a special type of link local address, the IPv4-compatible address obtained by prepending the null prefix 0:0:0:0:0:0 to the 32-bit IPv4 address.

96-bits	32-bits
0:0:0:0:0:0	IPv4 Address

— IPv4-compatible IPv6 Address Format —

The transmission rules and the transmission paths will depend on the direction of transmission.

7.3.1 Reaching the IPv6 Internet

Let's examine the case of an isolated IPv6 station X that uses its IPv4-compatible address to reach a fully connected IPv6 station Y. X must encapsulate its IPv6 packet in an IPv4 packet bound to an IPv6 router, in principle the nearest router in the routing domain. This router will decapsulate the IPv6 packet, which will then be forwarded toward its destination through IPv6 routing.

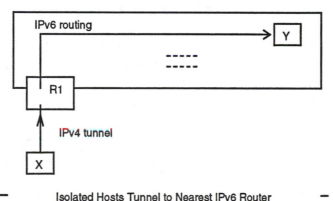

— Isolated Hosts Tunnel to Nearest IPv6 Router —

There are a few requirements for this procedure:

■ The isolated host must know the address of the IPv6 router.
■ The router must be ready to accept encapsulated packets and to forward them.
■ The tunnel must be correctly parameterized.

One could imagine that isolated IPv6 hosts get the address of the nearest router through some automatic configuration procedure, perhaps from a DHCP server. The IETF working group suggested the very elegant alternative of an IPv4 anycast address. One special address will be reserved in IPv4 to designate the IPv6 service. Routers capable of decapsulating IPv6 packets will announce a route toward that special address. Several routers may announce this route within one routing domain. Routing protocols will guarantee that tunneled packets will be delivered to the nearest one, which will be automatically backed up by the next nearest in case of failure.

Routers may indeed apply some checks before accepting to decapsulate and forward tunneled packets. They may, for example, verify that the IPv4 and IPv6 source addresses are consistent or that the IPv4 source is authorized and belongs to their routing domain.

7.3.2 Reaching Isolated Hosts

Those IPv6 hosts that are also IPv4 capable have no problem reaching isolated hosts. They will recognize that the destination address starts with the IPv4 prefix 0:0:0:0:0:0 and will immediately decide to encapsulate the IPv6 packet, to transmit it in an end-to-end IPv4 tunnel. The IPv4 destination address will be set to the last 32 bits of the IPv4-compatible address, the IPv4 source will be set to the IPv4 address of the outgoing interface.

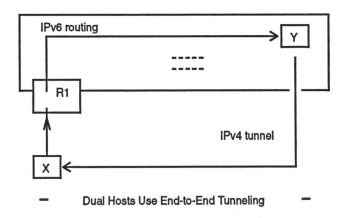

— Dual Hosts Use End-to-End Tunneling —

All dual hosts should be ready to receive encapsulated IPv6 packets. They are indeed not supposed to act as routers and thus should only silently discard those packets that are not bound to one of their IPv6 addresses.

We will eventually see the deployment of IPv6-only hosts that have no IPv4 connectivity. These hosts will simply pass the packets bound to the IPv6-compatible address to the nearest router, to be eventually forwarded to a dual router. This dual router will recognize that the IPv6 destination address starts with the prefix 0:0:0:0:0:0 and will automatically encapsulate it in an IPv4 packet bound to the final destination.

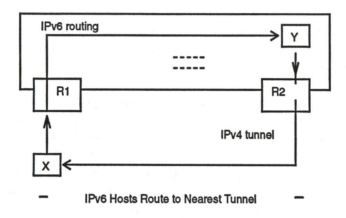

IPv6 Hosts Route to Nearest Tunnel

IPv4-capable IPv6 routers are expected to announce an IPv6 route toward the IPv4 address prefix in much the same way that IPv6-compatible IPv4 routers announce a route toward the reserved anycast address for tunnels.

The resulting routing is indeed asymmetric. In the direction from IPv6 to IPv4, the tunnel reaches the nearest IPv4 router, so most of the actual routing is done through IPv4. It would in fact be possible to announce routes for specific IPv4 networks in the IPv6 routing table. A router could, for example, announce that it serves the IPv4 local network designated by the IPv4 prefix 123.45.67/24 by announcing in IPv6 that it can reach ::123.45.67.0/120. But this would quickly lead to hyperinflation of the IPv6 routing table, the very devil that we are trying to put back in the box. The transition procedures do not mandate anything more than reachability of the basic IPv4 prefix.

7.3.3 MTU and TTL for Automatic Tunnels

The tunnels used to get packets to and from isolated hosts are not explicitly configured, yet one must choose IPv4 parameters such as the TTL or the MTU. In the case of the TTL, the generic recommendation that we mentioned previously still holds. Unless they know better, hosts should simply use the value recommended in the assigned numbers RFC of the day, currently 64 as per RFC 1700. The case of the MTU is more complex. In fact, we have to consider three cases:

- Isolated hosts managing a single tunnel toward the nearest IPv6 router
- Dual hosts managing tunnels toward their isolated partners
- Dual routers tunneling packets toward isolated hosts on behalf of IPv6-only hosts

Isolated hosts only manage one tunnel. They can run the MTU discovery procedure without any problem. Dual hosts should also be capable of running the MTU discovery procedures for all the currently active tunnels, although popular servers that have to answer to a large number of clients may find it difficult. Dual routers, on the other hand, may soon be faced with too many active tunnels to be able to effectively compute an MTU for each of them. They will always have the expedient to use the default minimum MTU of 576 octets and to authorize IPv4 fragmentation.

Routers that perform automatic tunneling may receive other error indications, notably ICMP unreachable messages. To avoid the black hole effect, they should try to translate these indications in an IPv6 ICMP message sent back to the IPv6 source.

The ICMP message includes the first byte of the discarded IPv4 packet. The first 20 bytes will be a copy of the encapsulating IPv4 header. The next 40 octets represent the original IPv6 header. If they are present, the router will use them to retrieve the original IPv6 source address, which could be used to construct an IPv6 ICMP error message.

7.3.4 Configurations and Decisions

We may expect that very shortly most Internet hosts will be equipped with IPv4 and IPv6 software. They will have to decide, for each connection or each UDP association, which version of the Internet Protocol they should use. The transition rules suggest that they will use IPv6 as often as possible, with one exception. If both stations are isolated, if the IPv6 address is in both cases derived from the IPv4

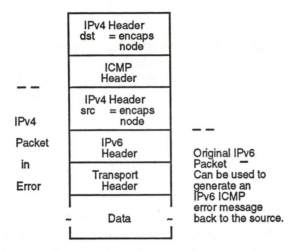

| IPv4 Header
dst = encaps
node |
| ICMP
Header |
| IPv4 Header
src = encaps
node |
| IPv6
Header |
| Transport
Header |
| Data |

IPv4 Packet in Error

Original IPv6 Packet – Can be used to generate an IPv6 ICMP error message back to the source.

IPv4 ICMP Error Message Returned to Encapsulating Node

address, using IPv6 would lead to the systematic use of an end-to-end tunnel in both directions.

IPv6 stations will have at least one IPv6 address registered in the DNS. When they want to reach a partner over the Internet, they will first ask the DNS for this partner's addresses, for example by using the AF_INET6 option of the hostname2addr command. If this command only returns IPv4 addresses, the connection will indeed be set up using IPv4. It the command only returns regular IPv6 addresses, the connection will obviously be set using IPv6. The decision is more difficult if the command returns only IPv4-compatible IPv6 addresses:

■ If the host is not connected to the IPv4 Internet, if it cannot reach an IPv4 router, it will have to use IPv6.

■ If the host discovers that the partner's IPv4-compatible address belongs to its local subnet, the two stations are on the same link and should use IPv6.

■ If the host is connected to the IPv4 Internet, it could use end-to-end tunnels, but should rather use a plain IPv4 connection to avoid the tunneling overhead.

IPv6-only stations, which do not have access to the IPv4 Internet, will indeed not be capable of communicating with IPv4-only stations.

7.4 Points of Controversy

The study of a transition strategy was as much plagued with controversy as the other points of the IPv6 design. Or maybe as rich in healthy debates. The hottest point of controversy regarded whether to support interoperation with IPv4-only nodes either before or after the doomsday when all IPv4 addresses will be allocated.

7.4.1 Should We Perform Translations?

The dual-stack decision was defined in the TUBA working group as a strategy for introducing CLNP in the Internet. At the same time, Robert Hinden and Dave Crocker were promoting inside the SIPP working group another approach to the problem, IP address encapsulation (IPAE). The single-stack approach of IPAE was considered for some time as a possible solution for IPv6. In IPAE, each host would have a single protocol stack, either IPv4 or IPv6. Those IPv6 hosts that were also configured with an IPv4 address could communicate with IPv4 hosts through header translation gateway. IPv4 addresses would be represented in the IPv6 format as *translatable addresses*.

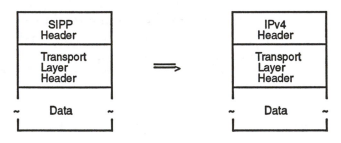

SIPP to IPv4 Header Translation according to IPAE

In the first iterations of the specification, the IPv6 translatable address was composed of a compatibility bit, a routing prefix, and a 32-bit IPv4 address. The routing prefix was in fact a function of the IPv4 network number, or rather CIDR prefix, designating for example the continent, the country, or the provider serving that particular network. This additional prefix would have been used to provide better aggregation capabilities and to reduce the size of the routing tables.

1	95-bits		32-bits
C	routing-prefix		IPv4 Address

—   IPv4-compatible IPv6 Address Format   —

The interoperability gateways would simply replace the IPv6 header by a corresponding IPv4 header, and vice versa. In one direction, the IPv4 source and destination addresses would be set to the last 32 bits of the IPv6 source and destination addresses; in the other direction the IPv6 addresses would be obtained by prepending to the IPv4 addresses the prefix corresponding to their network number. Changing the IPv4 header is almost transparent to transport protocols, except for the inclusion of source and destination addresses in TCP and UDP checksums through the pseudoheader. In one direction, the pseudoheader includes the 32-bit IPv4 addresses. In the other direction it should normally include the 128-bit addresses. This was the reason for including a C bit in the addresses for compatibility mode. The C bit is set when the address should be relayed by a translation gateway or was relayed by a translation gateway. If the bit is set, the UDP or TCP pseudoheaders should only include the IPv4 addresses.

But the IETF community did not accept the idea of a translation table sitting in every gateway. If such a table could be managed, then we would not need IPv6 in the first place, at least not for solving the IPv4 routing table explosion. We could as well give a copy of the table to every router, which would only have to compute routes for the upper layers of that table's hierarchy. Then, the idea of having special IPv4 checksum rules sitting forever in every TCP or UDP implementation was not particularly seductive.

80-bits	16-bits	32-bits
0:0:0:0:0	FFFF	IPv4 Address

—   IPv4-translatable IPv6 Address Format   —

In the last iteration of the specification, the translatable addresses were composed of the 96-bit prefix 0:0:0:0:0:FFFF followed by the 32-bit IPv4 address. Having a fixed prefix drastically simplified the management of the tables. The fact that this prefix summed to zero according to the TCP or UDP checksum rule removed the need for any special code in IPv6 implementations.

The translation approach was eventually rejected despite these simplifications. The details of the specification included too many little problems, such has how to translate fragmented IPv4 packets or how to handle source routed packets. Dual stack was going to be there in any case, because no serious manufacturer imagined that it could deliver a product in the coming years that would not support the current version of IP. The remaining problems could be solved by tunneling. Tunneling did perhaps induce somewhat more overhead than simple translation, but it was much easier to specify and debug, or at least so thought the majority of the IETF working group members.

7.4.2 Life after Doomsday

There will be a date, the doomsday of IPv4, when no more 32-bit addresses are available, or at least no more globally unique IPv4 addresses. At this moment, we will have

- IPv4-only hosts that can only be accessed through IPv4
- IPv6-only hosts that can only be accessed through IPv6
- Dual-stack hosts that can access both categories

The challenge is to arrive at that point in the best possible conditions, that is, with the least possible number of IPv4-only hosts. There are, however, two views here, the official one and the pessimist. According to the official estimations, we are almost sure to retain addresses until the year 2000, maybe 2008. The experimental deployment of IPv6 started in 1995 and will start to ramp up in 1996. Computers are generally replaced or upgraded every three years, which gives room for two cycles of equipment before doomsday. At that point, the only pockets of resistance will be very old machines, generally running in closed environments. The organizations owning these machines will probably organize their own private internet, for example using a local-use addressing plan based on network 10. The old machines will only be able to access local servers and to serve local clients, but that is a reasonable fate for outmoded machinery. We would never need any form of translation.

The pessimists retort that doomsday has already occurred. Many very large organizations would like to obtain a large number of addresses and cannot and thus must resort to building a private internet than only communicates with the worldwide Internet through some firewalls and other gateways. These organizations would benefit from very early conversion to IPv6, because they would have no difficulty obtaining a sufficient address space. In fact, they would benefit most if they could find products such as translating gateways that enable their IPv6-only stations to communicate immediately with IPv4-only hosts. It would be, in a sense, the revenge of the translation approach.

If there is customer demand for high-speed translation gateways, products are bound to appear. If these products support the translation between IPv4 and IPv6, then the conversion of the Internet to the new protocol will be accelerated.

7.5 Further Reading

Robert E. Gilligan and Erik Nordmark are currently preparing "Transition Mechanisms for IPv6 Hosts and Routers," which will soon be published as an RFC.

One design of a translation gateway is documented by P. Francis and K. Egevang, "The IP Network Address Translator (Nat)" in RFC 1631.

The use of reserved IP addresses to build up private Internet is documented by Y. Rekhter, R. Moskowitz, D. Karrenberg and G. de Groot in RFC 1597, "Address Allocation for Private Internets." It is discussed by E. Lear, E. Fair, D. Crocker, and T. Kessler in RFC 1627, "Network 10 Considered Harmful (Some Practices Shouldn't be Codified)."

A Provisional Conclusion

Alea jacta est. The dice have been rolled, the IPv6 specifications are available, implementors are busy implementing, and experimenters have started experimenting. The IPv6 solution won by consensus in the IETF, but this was a rough consensus. There are still pockets of resistance, dissatisfied competitors of the IPng race who tried to push other solutions, lost, and trying now to derail the IPv6 effort as being too little too soon. In their opinion, IPv6 is not a sufficient step forward. They hope to cling to IPv4 for some more years, a time that would be sufficient to research and develop a new product that would be, according to their wishes, much more powerful than IPv6. I am absolutely convinced, on the contrary, that IPv6 is the right solution at the right time.

8.1 The Right Solution

Transition is always a matter of carrots and sticks. Users, like stubborn donkeys, would only move from their actual comfortable position if they feared a big stick or if they were lured by a promising set of carrots. Listening to sour grapes, IPv6 does not provide enough of these carrots. The opponents of IPv6 discard neighbor discovery because IPv4's DHCP would be about as efficient; they discard security because it can be retrofitted in IPv4; they discard multicast because it is a mere extension of an existing IPv4 facility; and they discard the support of real time because ATM would do it better. They are wrong.

Neighbor discovery is not just a small step forward. Stateless address configuration requires much less management than manual configuration, or even DHCP. It is true that managers can insist on running DHCP for IPv6 as well as IPv4, in which case they will not benefit much from the new version. But neighbor discovery enables much more than the initial address configuration. A big difference between IPv4 and IPv6 is that IPv6 interfaces may be configured with several addresses. This allows organizations to connect to several providers at the same time, to arbitrage in real time between these providers. This facility is missing from IPv4, in which one interface usually only has one address. Even if we made the unrealistic assumption that all IPv4 softwares could be upgraded to support multiple addresses, we would quickly find that 32-bit addresses are running out faster if we give many of them to each station and we would need to move to IPv6 even sooner. It follows that provider addressing is realistic in IPv6, not in IPv4, despite CIDR.

The security payloads have been defined at the same time for both IPv4 and IPv6. It is thus true that we could obtain a secure Internet without having to move to IPv6. But integrating security into IPv4 requires a major system release, probably just as costly as a move to IPv6. If we bring up security, we may as well bring in IPv6 for about the same cost. This will be easier to manage, because security is mandated in IPv6 and will be present in all implementations, while it is only an optional add-on in IPv4.

The IPv6 protocol has the advantage of cleaning up many features of IPv4. The packet format is better aligned, unused fields have been removed, the header extensions are easier to use than IPv4 options. The IPv6 support for multicast is typical here in two respects. First, the support for multicast will be present from day 1 in all IPv6 implementations, while it has yet to be fully integrated in many IPv4 stacks seven years after the publication of RFC 1112 and three years after the deployment of the MBone. Second, the inclusion of a scope field in the IPv6 multicast addresses will remove one of the worst management nightmares in IPv4 multicast, the overloading of a scope control function in the TTL. We should no longer see students misconfiguring the TTL parameter in their interfaces and swamping the whole Internet with a high-definition video transmission of their laboratory.

Some would have liked to base the real-time support in the Internet on a flow model, nearer to ATM virtual circuits than IP datagrams. I am glad that Steve Deering resisted their pressure. The inclusion of flow labels and drop priorities in IPv6 is adequate for supporting modern multimedia applications. The bulk of future multimedia exchanges will be supported by adaptive applications that benefit most from the transmission efficiency and the multiplexing gains of datagram networks, especially when combined with fair queuing and the selective drops that IPv6's drop priority support enables. We should, in fact, see very little of the rigid real-time applications for which ATM virtual circuits were designed 10 years ago. These rigid applications will in any case be able to use reservation protocols, in combination with IPv6 labeling of flows.

IPv6 keeps most of the original Internet Protocol design, and this is a good thing. We avoided most of the second-design syndrome, and the specification is not bloated with gratuitous changes. But we did insert those changes that were justified by 15 years of experience, and we obtained a very good solution.

8.2 The Right Time

The sour grapes discourse not only mentions the lack of carrots, it also mentions the lack of stick. If we prolongate the current curves of address allocation as a function of time, our pen crosses over the 32-bit addressing ceiling some 10 or 20 years after the end of the century. Some will take this as a scientific result and deduce that we do not need to change IPv4 for at least 10 years. They are wrong.

Large companies would very much like to get a class A IPv4 network number so that they could obtain enough address space to organize their internal network into a hierarchy of subnets, sites, and confederations of regions. But the current address allocation policies are so Malthusian that they cannot even get a class B number. They take great pains trying to use a small block of CIDR prefixes. The result is that the Internet does not grow as fast as it could.

CIDR makes the hidden assumption that prefixes belong to a provider hierarchy. This is the condition for routing tables to scale. Customers switch providers to get better services and keep their prefixes to avoid the pain of renumbering. Competition is such that their new providers have to agree to advertise these old prefixes. The result is that the routing tables are getting more and more out of hand.

Even if Malthusian CIDR allocations do trim the Internet's growth, they cannot stop it entirely. We will be running out of class C numbers within a year or two, and we will have to start allocating slices of class A numbers to the new customers. This does not quite correlate with the prediction of a long-lasting 32-bit address space.

Deploying IPv6, on the contrary, ensures that we can grow the Internet at an even faster rate, without having to fear the exhaustion of address space or the explosion of routing tables. The first alpha releases of the software have already been tested, the first beta releases will be distributed by the end of 1995, and commercial distribution will start in 1996. This is just the right time to start the transition, well before we bump our noses on the limitations of the current 32-bit address space.

8.3 The Future Will Tell

It is hard to predict the future. IPv6 was born under good auspices, a well-gifted protocol with attentive elders. But we do not know yet whether it will succeed, which is why I consider that this chapter can only be a provisional conclusion to the presentation of IPv6. In between, I invite you to meditate on the course of time and history. Who would have thought, in 1978, when the personal computer was not yet invented, that there would be so many millions of hosts in the Internet that we would urgently need to deploy a new version, with an increased address space?

Glossary

Acronyms are a necessary evil. They puzzle newcomers and they render texts hermetic and esoteric. Yet they are unavoidable in a technical specification. I have tried to list here all the acronyms that I used, as well as the most important key words relating to the new Internet protocol.

AAAA

The type of records holding IPv6 addresses in the domain name service.

AF_INET

The type of current IP addresses in the UNIX socket library.

AF_INET6

The type of the new IPv6 addresses in the UNIX socket library.

AH

Authentication header.

Anycast

Sending to the nearest member of a group of servers.

API

Application programming interface.

APNIC

Asia-Pacific Network Information Center.

Appletalk

Network protocol used by Apple computers.

ARP

Address Resolution Protocol (in IPv4).

ATM

Automatic teller machine (for banks). Asynchronous transfer mode (for telecommunication companies), or another terrible mistake.

Autonomous System

In IPv4, a set of connected networks with an independent administration.

BGP

Border Gateway Protocol, used for routing between autonomous systems.

Black hole

A network configuration that absorb packets without any noise or light.

BSD

The version of the UNIX system developed by Berkeley University.

CATNIP

One of the candidate proposals for IPng.

CIDR

Classless interdomain routing.

CLNP

Connectionless Network Protocol, defined by the ISO.

Dartnet

A research network, financed by DARPA, where several extensions to IP were tested.

DES

Data Encryption Standard.

DES-CBC

Data Encryption Standard, used in cipher block chaining mode.

DHCP

Dynamic Host Configuration Protocol.

Diffie–Hellman

A zero-knowledge key exchange algorithm proposed by Whitfield Diffie and Martin Hellman.

DNS

Domain name service. The distributed database that stores the addresses of Internet hosts and other data.

DSS

Digital Signature Standard, defined by NIST or U.S. federal users.

Dual stack

Qualification of hosts that can run two sets of network protocols in parallel (e.g., IPv4 and IPv6).

EGP

Exterior Gateway Protocol.

EIGRP

Extended version of cisco's IGRP protocol.

ES-IS

End System to Intermediate System Routeing Protocol. Provides the equivalent of neighbor discovery for CNLP.

ESP

Encrypted security payload.

FIPS

Federal Information Processing Standard.

Firefly

The name of a classified key exchange protocol designed by the NSA.

Firewall

A computer used to filter access to an organization's network.

FTP

File Transfer Protocol.

Gethostbyname

A procedure used by IPv4 applications to get addresses of named partners.

Hackers

In the old days, a hacker was a very clever programmer. Today's hackers use their art to get unauthorized access through the network.

HBH

Hop by hop options.

Hostname2addr

Replacement of gethostbyname for IPv6.

H ratio

A notation of address allocation efficiency.

HTTP

HyperText Transport Protocol, used for accessing World-Wide Web servers.

IAB

Internet Architecture Board (was Internet Activities Board until 1992).

IANA

Internet Assigned Numbers Authority.

ICMP

Internet Control Message Protocol.

ICMPv6

ICMP for IPv6.

IDEA

An encryption algorithm, used in the Pretty Good Privacy package.

IDPR

Interdomain Policy Routing Protocol.

IDRP

Interdomain Routing Protocol.

IEEE-802

A committee of the IEEE that published standards for local networks. The 48-bit address format defined by that committee.

IESG

Internet Engineering Steering Group.

IETF

Internet Engineering Task Force.

IGMP

Internet Group Management Protocol for IPv4. Subsumed by ICMP in IPv6.

IGP

Interior Gateway Protocol.

IGRP

Cisco's Interior Gateway Routing Protocol.

IHL

Internet Header Length in IPv4.

INRIA

The French National Institute for Computer Science and Control.

INTERNIC

The Internet's Network Information Center.

IP

Internet Protocol

IPAE

IP address encapsulation, a transition technique once envisaged for migrating to IPv6.

IP in IP

One of the early proposals for IPng.

IPng

IP new generation. The official name of the not yet defined new protocol until the July 1994 decision.

IPv4

IP version 4, the current version of IP.

IPv4 compatible

An IPv4 address in IPv6 format.

IPv4 only

A host that cannot run IPv6.

IPv6

IP version 6, the new version of IP.

IPv6 only

A host that cannot run IPv4.

IPX

A network protocol defined by Novell.

IS-IS

Intermediate System to Intermediate System Routing Protocol, defined by the ISO for CLNP; also used in some IP networks.

ISO

The International Organization for Standards.

ISO-IP

An old designation of CLNP.

ISO-TP4

ISO Transport Protocol Class 4.

ITU

International Telecommunication Union.

IVS

Inria Videoconferencing System.

kbps

Kilobits per second

kHz

Kilohertz.

Keyed-MD5

A signature computation algorithm used with the authentication header.

Link local

Qualification of addresses that are only valid on a single link.

LZ77

A compression algorithm defined by Lempel and Ziv in 1977.

LZS

A further refinement of LZ77.

MBONE

The experimental multicast backbone, an overlay network deployed over the Internet to test multicast applications.

Mbps

Megabits per second.

MD2, MD4, MD5

Message-digest algorithms. These one way functions are used to compute cryptographic checksums.

MPEG

Moving Picture Expert Group. The video compression algorithm defined by this group.

MTU

Media transmission unit.

Multicast

Sending to a selected group at once, in opposition to broadcast, which reaches everybody, and unicast, which reaches only one target.

NBMA

Nonbroadcast multiple access. A network that provides connectivity but does not support multicast.

NCC

Network Coordination Center (of RIPE).

NFS

Network file system.

NIC

Network Information Center.

NSA

U.S. National Security Agency.

NSAP

Network service access point address.

NTP

Network Time Protocol.

OSI

Open System Interconnection. A networking architecture, the seven layer models, and many related standards defined by ISO.

OSPF

Open shortest path first. An IGP for both IPv4 autonomous systems and IPv6 routing domains.

Pad1

A one-octet padding option in the option headers.

PadN

> A multiple-octet padding option in the option headers.

PC

> Personal computer.

PDU

> Protocol data unit. The ISO name for a message or a packet.

PF_INET

> The IPv4 protocol family in the socket library.

PF_INET6

> The IPv6 protocol family in the socket library.

PGP

> Pretty good privacy. A software package enabling users to encrypt their files and their mail messages.

Photuris

> The Greek name for a firefly. A key exchange protocol proposed for securing IPv4 and IPv6.

Ping

> A program that uses the ICMP echo function to test reachability of peers.

Pip

> Paul's internet protocol. A protocol proposed by Paul Francis as a candidate IPng solution.

PPP

> Point to point protocol, used for exchanging IP datagram and other data over serial links.

Quadrillion

> We use the North American definition, a thousand million millions. IPv6 is defined to support a quadrillion hosts.

RAP

> A routing protocol, part of the TP/IX proposal.

RC2, RC4

> Encryption algorithms.

Renater

> The IP network that links French universities and research institutes.

RFC

Request for comment. The name of the archival publications of the IAB and IETF.

RH

Routing header.

RIP

Route Information Protocol. A RIPng is being defined for IPv6.

RIPE

Réseaux IP Européens. The association of European IP networks.

Routeing

The ISO spelling for *routing*.

RSA

An asymmetric encryption algorithm that allows users to publish their public key. From the name of the inventors, Rivest, Shamir, and Adleman.

RSVP

Resource Reservation Protocol for IPv4 and IPv6.

SDR

Source demand routing. A working group of the IETF.

SDRP

Source Demand Routing Protocol.

SHA

A one-way function used to compute cryptographic checksums in the DSS.

SIGCOMM

The Computer Communication special interest group of the ACM.

SIP

Simple IP, or Steve's IP. Steve Deering's original proposal for IPng.

SIPP

Simple IP Plus. The result of the merging between SIP and Pip. IPv6 is based on SIPP.

SMTP

Simple Mail Transfer Protocol.

SNA

IBM's System Network Architecture.

SNMP

Simple Network Management Protocol.

Socket

The system interface used by UNIX BSD applications to access network services.

Sonet

A U.S. standard that defines a hierarchy of transmission rates for high-speed digital circuits. The international equivalent is SDH, synchronous digital hierarchy.

SPI

Security parameter index. Used to identify a security association.

ST

Stream Protocol.

T1

A 1.5-Mbps digital circuit. Europeans would use E1 circuits at 2 Mbps.

T3

A 45-Mbps digital circuit. Europeans would use E3 circuits at 34 Mbps.

TBD

To be defined.

TCP

Transport control protocol.

TCP-IP

Often used to identify the whole networking technology developed around TCP and IP.

TOS

Type of service, in IPv4.

TP/IX

One of the early candidates for IPng, proposed by Robert Ullman.

Trillion

We use the North American definition, million millions. IPv6 is designed to support a trillion networks.

Triple DES

> An algorithm in which the DES is run three times for stronger resistance to decryption attacks.

TTL

> Time to live. The time a packet is allowed to spend in the network.

TUBA

> TCP and UDP over Bigger Address. The proposal to use CLNP for IPng. The acronym was forged by Ross Callon.

UDP

> User Datagram Protocol.

Unicast

> A transmission towards exactly one destination.

UNIX

> An operating system, very popular on the Internet.

INDEX